The Poetry
of Sara Pujol Russell

Sara Pujol Russell

The Poetry
of Sara Pujol Russell

Translated and with an Introduction
by Noël Valis

SUP

Selinsgrove: Susquehanna University Press

Associated University Presses
2010 Eastpark Boulevard
Cranbury, NJ 08512

The paper used in this publication meets the requirements of the American National Standard for Permanence of Paper for Printed Library Materials Z39.48-1984.

Library of Congress Cataloging-in-Publication Data

Pujol Russell, Sara.
  [Poems. English & Spanish. Selections]
  The poetry of Sara Pujol Russell / translated and with an introduction by Noël Valis.
      p.   cm.
  Includes bibliographical references.
  ISBN 1-57591-099-3
  1. Pujol Russell, Sara—Translations into English.   I. Valis, Noël Maureen, 1945–   II. Title.

PQ6716.U3A28   2005
861'.7—dc22

                                                            2005044238

PRINTED IN THE UNITED STATES OF AMERICA

Contents

Introduction   9

A Note on the Translation   19

Selected Bibliography   21

From: *El fuego tiende su aire* • *Fire Floats its Air*   24

  Contemplación primera • First Contemplation   24

  Tiempo de luz, tiempo de agua • Time of Light, Time of Water   26

  La noche me llama sereno aire, sereno sueño • Night Calls
     Me Serene Air, Serene Sleep   28

  Origen del verbo, germinación de la tierra • Origin of
     the Word, Flowering of the Earth   30

  Con las manos sobre la ausencia • With my Hands
     upon Absence   32

  Aroma de mirra, aroma de soledad • The Smell of Myrrh,
     the Smell of Solitude   34

  Mi desnudez es olor a sueños • My Being Naked is the
     Smell of Dreams   36

  Vivir en palabra callada • To Live in the Silent Word   38

  Como ciervo que bebe el silencio de la rosa • Like a Deer
     Drinking the Silence of the Rose   40

  Creación de mi nombre • Creation of my Name   42

  Soledad de piedra • Solitude of Stone   44

  Soledad de luna • Solitude of Moon   46

  Interpretación de la rosa • Interpretation of the Rose   48

  Angustia sosegada • The Comfort of Anguish   50

  Oración al atardecer • A Prayer at Dusk   52

  Tú, caminante • You, Traveler   54

  Conocimiento de la primavera • Knowing Spring   56

  Si es de noche y te sorprende • If it's Night and
     It Surprises You   58

De aire la vida • Out of Air, Life 60

Septiembre • September 62

Enséñame • Teach me 64

Soledad • Solitude 66

Sencillez • Simplicity 68

Si pudiera • If I Could Only 70

Pensar la tarde • Thinking Late Afternoon 72

Silencio • Silence 74

Historia de abril. Entonces • April History. Then 76

From: *Intacto asombro en la luz del silencio* • *Astonishment
Intact in the Light of Silence* 78

Dominio del recuerdo • Dominion of Memory 78

Amor, hondura de la sed • Love, Deep Thirst 80

Un cuerpo, el sur • A Body, the South 82

Recogido asombro • Quiet Astonishment 84

Como mayo, el ser se acerca • Like May, Life Approaches 86

Canción de aroma • Scent Song 88

A veces, el presente es • Sometimes, Now Is 90

El tiempo distinto de cada ausencia • A Different Time in
Every Absence 92

Cerrar para abrir • To Enclose is to Open 94

Pared blanca, fluyo en voz por vuestro silencio • White Wall,
I Flow in the Voice Because of Your Silence 96

La luz entra por el verso • Light Enters through Poetry 98

Cierre del ciclo de la nieve • Closing the Cycle of Snow 100

Cerco seco de mi nombre • Dry Circle of my Name 102

Tuviste mapas de otros ríos • You Had Maps of Other Rivers 104

Empiezo donde empieza la palabra • I Begin Where the
Word Begins 108

Loto y rosa en la flor azul • Lotus and Rose in the Blue Flower 110

Todo huele a silencio • Everything Smells Like Silence 112

Coda: 114

Con el corazón desmesurado me tiendo en la luz • With a
Boundless Heart I Stretch out in the Light 114

¿Qué la eternidad? Sólo conozco la carencia • What About
    Eternity? I Know Only Lack   116
Aunque todo se incumpla, se cumple el aire • Though Nothing
    is Fulfilled, the Air is Filled   118
Creación del silencio • Creation of Silence   120
Cuando algo tiende a lo absoluto • When Something
    Tends to the Absolute   122

Introduction

DOES POETRY HAVE A LIFE? CAN WE PLOT ITS COURSE, MARK OFF deaths and anniversaries, point out the houses it has lived in, the lovers it has had, the failures and successes? In one sense, of course, such questions are unthinkable because absurd. In another, though, they are unthinkable because we generally *do not* think about them. Poets have lives. Readers have lives. A poem may have a publishing life in the way it is received and read, in the way it influences other poems, but a life? Suppose, however, the possibility of such a life. What would it be like?

It might be like Sara Pujol Russell's poetry. Consider, for example, a poem called "Like May, Life Approaches":

> Like May, life approaches the word and, incessant,
> the word seeks life, birds streaming, love flaming,
> the scent of the river, a body tendering dreams of time.
> Life and word are the same then: a long silence in the grass.
> Let me, silence, be like the word—a dance of fire—
> and let the word be like me—a dance of water in the grass.

Like all her poems, this one is extraordinary for the density of presence, for its lyrical complexity. This is highly conceptualized, metaphysical poetry that challenges us to unwrap her imagery word for word and thus to enter intimately into her special poetic universe. Such poetry relies less on narrative and more on the compulsion of words themselves. As Pujol herself remarks, "the anecdote is not important—it only interests me insofar as it is the celebration of the heart in flames, as a festival of reason leaning into its own ardor—if it is vital experience surpassing its own circumstance, if it is spiritual life transcending its own limitations, if it is an interpretation of being and existing in the world" (2001, 116).

"Like May, Life Approaches" does not possess a biography. But there is life. In translating this poem, I have taken liberties. The poet uses the word "ser," or "being," rather than "life" and yet, I think we

9

can call being "life" here. Pujol does not say, of course, poetry is life, or even that her poem *has* a life, but I would argue that it does, in the way that word and life, or being, are two elements of the same thing. The poem is enigmatic: why should life, like May, approach the word? The first three lines are like a flow of life in the word. Life moves toward the word. The word is incessant, birds streaming, love flaming, the scent of a river, a body tendering dreams of time. Everything is in movement, like May. Conventionally May could stand for spring and the renewal of life, but this poem only starts with that notion in order to suggest something else, something more.

There is a natural, abrupt stop after the words "Like May," perhaps to emphasize the conventional image of spring, but then the poem begins to move, to flow. The opening line seems to personalize life, May, and the word itself through the use of such verbs as "approaches" and "seeks." At the same time, the device of prosopopoeia, or personification, is only approximate, for life is not May, it is a simile, an expressed comparison that stresses a certain similarity and contiguity between life and May. Pujol makes that contiguity intimate, not only in the placement of words but in the choice of verbs.

I find this remarkable, the way in which she takes something abstract—life (*el ser*), the word (not *a* word)—and turns it into something intimate (see also Peñas-Bermejo). The repetition of certain sounds in the original—the p's of *palabra* (word), the sibilant s's of *ser, se, incesante,* the a's of *arroyo* (stream) and *aves* (birds)—works in the same direction of closing the metaphysical distance inherent to her conceptualizing and zooming in on life, or being, itself. I have tried to approximate what could be called this intimate flow by creating compensatory similarities of sound in the l's of "like" and "life," the s's of "incessant," "seeks," and "streaming," and by using the present participle forms of "streaming," "flaming," and "tendering," but my efforts must remain loving simulacra of the original.

Despite this sense of intimacy, "May" remains mysterious, like the entire poem. Pujol makes even more complex the meaning of these lines when she slides from approximation to identification in saying: "Life and word are the same then: a long silence in the grass." In one line she tries to erase, or at least alter, the fundamental distinction between language and the real, or being. This move appears in many of her poems. The title of one condenses her poetic strategy: "Origin of the Word, Flowering of the Earth." Another is called "To Live in the Silent Word." She ends the poem "Knowing Spring" thus: "flow has the name of spring." In another, September "breaks the wound and flees, in love, from name to name" ("September"). The same idea is implicit to lines like these: "How to be more and not be something else if my life already is opening / into doves as though my face, and my home already has a river, a name? / Light enters through poetry, and body, soul, and afternoon have changed" ("Light Enters through Poetry"). And in "I Begin Where the Word Begins," she writes:

> The word begins like a deer in a mouth, like a fountain
> in the grass, like fire in air, like air in dreams,
> like earth and flame in the mouth of the deer, like a stone
> in cherries, like water in firs, like water and field
> in the voice, in the uncertainty of the certain voice,
> like pain transcended, or eyes, like a dream unconsummated,
> like time consummated, like compliant silence.

The poem ends in this way: "Word, I find salvation in you only where I begin like a deer, / like a fountain, like a dream in the clearest certainty."

The dream of poetry is to be life. In Sara Pujol, poetry dreams. It dreams like May, it flows in dreams of time, in the scent of the river, in the long silence of the grass. In this dream of "clearest certainty," then, life and word are one. The poet makes a further identification by saying: "Let me, silence, be like the word—a dance of fire—/ and let the word be like me—a dance of water in the grass." Here, Pujol plays with two of the traditional elements comprising the universe: fire and water, which are linked to the earlier images of birds streaming, love flaming, and the scent of the river. The four elements in varying combinations appear in other poems as well. For example, in "Out of Air, Life" we read: "Be silent and breathe / with the harmony of fire your life of air, only air."

As Julia Uceda perceptively observes, this pre-Socratic vision of union is re-elaborated as a kind of dynamic circularity in Sara Pujol's poetry, starting with the dual naming of *El fuego tiende su aire* (Fire Floats its Air), which on the dorso of the book reads: *El aire tiende a su fuente* (Air Floats its Fountain) (2003, 25). (The device of the doubled title is also used for *Intacto asombro en la luz del silencio / El silencio del loto, la luz de las rosas* [Astonishment Intact in the Light of Silence / The Silence of the Lotus, the Light of Roses].) This doubling back does not signify the myth of the eternal return, but a different kind of vision which is difficult to name, as Uceda remarks (2003, 25). Manuel Mantero calls her poetry "anomalous" in its beauty and strangeness (1999, 115; 118).

11

Rather, one senses a profound permeability of interchangeable realities in her poetry. Thus, the lyrical voice of "Like May, Life Approaches" asks to "be like the word—a dance of fire" and the word to "be like me—a dance of water in the grass." Each "dance" does not simply reflect back to the other one, but establishes mutual analogies, as though fire and water could ultimately merge one into the other, becoming something else that does not have a name yet. In some respects, Pujol's vision could be called pantheistic, as when she writes in one of her loveliest poems, "Scent Song":

Summer. Suddenly I am May, with April
still in my hands. I am more May than May and more time than time itself.
I am the slow wind that rocks the trees, and the trees
are me, steady and tender, a dense air-born now,
and I am a fragile sensing, pleasure and pain inside feeling
and sad, habitual thought trembling in the stone-light.

With its May motif, this poem also echoes the previous one, "Like May, Life Approaches." In this case, the lyrical voice is "more May than May." She is the slow wind, the trees steady and tender, and time itself. But romantic pantheism, which identifies God and nature, seems inadequate if not misleading when speaking of Sara Pujol's poetry. The sense of transcendent being is clearly immanent here, indwelling in the poetic subject (see Peñas-Bermejo). More significantly, Pujol stresses heightened sensations that in themselves seem to create a universe of the permeable, rather than the other way around. Thus, she is "the *slow* wind that *rocks* the trees"; she is "a *dense* air-born *now*" (my emphases). She is "a fragile sensing, pleasure and pain inside feeling / and sad, habitual thought trembling in the stone-light." This intensity of sensation takes abstract, generalized words like pleasure, pain, feeling, and thought and forces us to see them in a more personal way.

The odd coincidence of the individual and the universal in the same words is characteristic of her poetry. Pujol's poetry undoubtedly has its roots in romantic subjectivity, but the philosophical frame takes it into another realm: into the universal of the universe. This is what I mean by the universal character of her poetry: the permeability of things, the sense that everything seems to slip into everything else, creates not only Pujol's own particular universe, but *the* universe insofar as the poetic objects of her poetry constitute a universal sphere. In "Scent Song" the poet says:

Suddenly, I am no longer that love looking inside the tanners'
earthen jars, but love looking at itself,
that names and measures itself in acacias, that names and gives me sleep.
Summer, and I am a slow walking in May, pure child,
a serene walking in scents and love on my lips.

First, she gives us love in its particularities: "love looking inside the
tanners' earthen jars," then love, more universally, "looking at itself." Is
it the mere reflection of love that looks into the tanners' earthen jars, in
contrast to the directness of love seeing itself, naming and measuring?
I am not sure how to answer my own question, only to say that there is
something I find personally captivating about this ancient image of the
tanners'earthen jars turning up, like mysterious verbal artifacts, in
these extremely modern verses. Whatever love is in this poem, it can-
not be separated from the rest of the poem's images and sensations. The
last two lines—"Summer, and I am a slow walking in May, pure child /
a serene walking in scents and love on my lips"—in which Pujol distills
the essence of "Scent Song," make that clear.

In line with this sense of permeable inseparability, she creates a net-
work of imagery that connects (and even generates) the poems themat-
ically and structurally. Thus we find echoes of the same lines between
poems. In the first poem of *Astonishment Intact*, "Dominion of Mem-
ory," the line, "the dream of an orange tree become a man and a sweet
word in flames" ("del sueño de ser naranjo hecho hombre y dulce verbo
en llamas"), reappears in "A Body, the South." The last line of "Quiet
Astonishment" contains the phrase "life approaches the word" ("el ser
se acerca a la palabra"), which appears as the first line in the very next
poem, "Like May, Life Approaches." And the last poem, "Everything
Smells Like Silence," begins "So it is winter" ("Y es invierno") and
ends with "It is winter, the word burns serene and everything smells
like silence" ("Es invierno, el verbo arde sereno y todo huele a silen-
cio"), thus linking this poem to the first one of the collection, which be-
gins: "Remembering is always a long winter slowly opening the wheat"
("Recordar es siempre un invierno largo abriendo lento el trigo") ("Do-
minion of Memory"). The long, incantatory lines and the lyrical rush of
imagery embrace the universe, even its pain and absences. This is ec-
static poetry, as astonishing as the title of *Intacto asombro / Astonish-
ment Intact* suggests.

The ecstatic quality of her poetry—its out-of-stateness—is closely
associated with another condition, which she names "nostalgia" and I

have translated as "longing." The poem, "My Being Naked is the Smell of Dreams," exquisitely expresses this feeling, which is also a series of sensations in Pujol's vision of things:

> Longing is an ivory precipice, a thick quiver of dreams,
> the past's brocaded night, the future's burning mouth,
> the heart beating like oars against air, water, earth, blood,
> the sense of permanence, solitude in the five senses:
> when everything is longing you end up longing nothing,
> you live naked, broken on the rack, open only to the fragrant trace.

Nostalgia, as I have commented elsewhere, "is, metaphorically and affectively, truly something out of place, operating as a narrative of loss and memory and centered on a phantom topography of desire." Susan Stewart says simply that "nostalgia is the desire for desire." The first line of "My Being Naked is the Smell of Dreams"—"Longing is an ivory precipice, a thick quiver of dreams"—reminds us of the deep connection between longing and dreams. Her "ivory precipice" may be an echo of Homer, who says:

> Many and many a dream is mere confusion,
> a cobweb of no consequence at all.
> Two gates for ghostly dreams there are: one gateway
> of honest horn, and one of ivory.
> Issuing by the ivory gate are dreams
> of glimmering illusion, fantasies,
> but those that come through solid polished horn
> may be borne out, if mortals only know them.[1]

The ivory gate leads to illusions and fantasies, horn to solid realities. Pujol's longing—her nostalgia—plunges into the precipice of dream. The senses appear to come richly alive in dreams: in the brocaded night of the past, the burning mouth of the future, in the heart beating like oars against air, water, earth, blood. The very title of the poem—"My Being Naked is the Smell of Dreams"—mixes dream and desire together, slipping the senses into dream, turning dream into *jouissance*, "longing for the moving form, / the sensual longing for abundance, joy, delight / and desire," as she says later in the same poem.

Pujol's longing is universal to the extent that longing covers, it absorbs, yearns for everything out there. It is, she says in the same poem, "pure longing that will not yield to the sun of time." The longing she feels is "to bathe in all the fountains and waters / full of stars, horizons and the green circles of golden hours"; "to drink rain and more rain, to be / a river among rivers and clusters of ice and fog in the woods." The poem ends with these words: "Longing, precipice of the moon, burning quiver night after night, / I am open nakedness, bright coals, with a single smell of dreams."

The dream of poetry, I said before, is to be life. "My Being Naked is the Smell of Dreams" shows that dream is the source *for* life, a source that is neither constant nor reliable. Thus Pujol writes: "Sometimes, you would like to feel longing, the deep well of longing / for an absence, for a child who is the flowering tree, a pain which is the sea, / for a river, a caress in the pearl drop of the moon . . . but you do not feel it." This dream of life, which in literature has ancient roots, has depth and longitude—it is a "deep well" and "pain which is the sea"—but is concentrated in the universe of a single individual. It is not necessarily an individual called Sara Pujol Russell. When I asked her for a bio, she replied: "A bio? I only have the stuff that appears in the inside flap of my books." There we learn that she was born in Barcelona, has a doctorate, and teaches Spanish literature at the Universitat Rovira i Virgili in Tarragona. She works in contemporary poetry and literary theory, has done translation, is chief editor of the journal *Salina*, and co-director, with Julia Uceda, of the collection, *La Barca de Loto*, published by Esquío. In 1980, she won the Recull Prize for *Inquietud di pleniluni*. Her poetry has appeared in Catalan and Spanish and has been translated into Italian, French, Lithuanian, Portuguese, and Chinese. But none of this helps to situate her poetry, which does not fall easily into any school of writing. The closest she comes to is Julia Uceda's poetry, which is also metaphysical and centered on the passion for, and of, being, but neither is Pujol a disciple of Uceda nor is Uceda representative of a particular literary movement.[2]

More significantly, the dream of poetry to be life has little to do with the conventional biography of a writer. Had I highlighted these biographical details earlier it would make no difference in understanding poems like "My Being Naked is the Smell of Dreams." It would make no difference. The universe of a single individual that this and other Pujol poems encapsulate is larger than Pujol herself, as the lyrical voice in "My Being Naked" tells us, in its longing for "beauty . . . living apart from my troubled gaze, / from my defeated silence, from my defeated hands thrust in the flames." She needs "to be love in love, love that never / stretches to the past, the rose that never contemplates the fleet-

15

ing." To be, as the last line of the poem affirms, "open nakedness, bright coals, with a single smell of dreams." This "single smell of dreams" in its nakedness suggests that Homer's ivory gate of illusion has in some sense merged with the gate of horn in Pujol's poetry. The reality of the senses ("the sense of permanence, solitude in the five senses"), of sensations ("open nakedness, bright coals"), is the dream that "may be borne out," as Homer puts it, "if mortals only know [such dreams]," for dreams pass through *both* gates. And by implication in Pujol's poem, dreams may be borne out, brought to life, if only we can catch the "smell of dreams." At the same time, "when everything is longing you end up longing nothing," because this totality of longing swallows up the specific, the finite, turning them into a universe of longing.

In "A Body, the South," Pujol writes:

> So much well-taught wine on the tongue resounds in rivers,
> so much wine descending from thirst, from walls of lime,
> from the south forever questioning lips or resting in a kiss,
> the south—full moon in a mouth, Circe of light, Circe of time—
> forever plunging the mouth, light, time, the kiss in the earth
> and the earth rises for man and man returns to dreams.

Here again are echoes of Homer, resounding in the enchantress's name of Circe, who turned men into pigs. The dream of poetry to be life can only come from the transformative delights of enchantment, symbolized in the "south—full moon in a mouth, Circe of light, Circe of time—/ forever plunging the mouth, light, time, the kiss in the earth / and the earth rises for man and man returns to dreams." So too does poetry.

NOTES

1. See Noël Valis, *The Culture of Cursilería: Bad Taste, Kitsch and Class in Modern Spain* (Durham: Duke University Press, 2002), 244; Susan Stewart, *On Longing: Narratives of the Miniature, the Gigantic, the Souvenir, the Collection* (Baltimore: Johns Hopkins University Press, 1984), 23; and Homer, *The Odyssey*, trans. Robert Fitzgerald (Garden City, NY: Doubleday and Company, 1963), 371.

2. For more on Uceda (National Prize for Poetry, 2003), see *The Poetry of Julia Uceda*, trans. and introd. Noël Valis (New York: Peter Lang, 1995); and Uceda's *En el viento, hacia el mar, 1959–2002*, ed. and prol. Sara Pujol Russell (Seville: Fundación José Manuel Lara, 2002). In "Los gozos de la contemplación," Biruté Ciplijauskaité places Pujol Russell's work within the broad category of contemplative poetry (in *The*

16

Discovery of Poetry: Essays in Honor of Andrew P. Debicki, ed. Roberta Johnson [Boulder: Society of Spanish and Spanish-American Studies, 2003], 155–71). See also her "Criatura frente a la creación," *Salina* 14 (2000): 159–68; and "Desde la marginalidad hacia el centro a través de la palabra," in *Identidades culturales*, ed. María Ángeles Hermosilla Álvarez and Amalia Pulgarín Cuadrado (Córdoba: Universidad de Córdoba, 2001), 224–25 esp. Pujol would probably subscribe to these words of Mordecai Roshwald: "contemplation . . . supersedes reality. Reality . . . slips through our consciousness like sand through our fingers, while the objects of contemplative experience retain their essence and remain imperishable" ("Reality and Contemplation," *Modern Age* 46, nos. 1–2 [2004]: 62). For other views of Pujol Russell's poetry, see the Selected Bibliography below.

A Note on the Translation

THIS SELECTION OFFERS A REPRESENTATIVE SAMPLING OF PUJOL'S poetry from her two collections in Spanish: *El fuego tiende su aire / El aire tiende a su fuente* and *Intacto asombro en la luz del silencio / El silencio del loto, la luz de las rosas*. Some of these poems originally appeared in Catalan, in *Lentitud d'hivern* (1997): "Contemplación primera" ("Matí de febrer. Migdia. El temps no s'ha succeït"), "Tiempo de luz, tiempo de agua" ("Llum, l'aigua d'una font que no existeix"), "La noche me llama sereno aire, sereno sueño" ("Nit. Fosca nit. Serenitat. Res no em torba. Serenitat"), "Origen del verbo, germinación de la tierra" ("¡Oh, dolç atzar, que tries, sense caprici, l'hora"), and "Con las manos sobre la ausencia" ("Arribarà la nit i pensaré en què he pasta el dia"). Thus, in some cases, Pujol's later versions in Spanish have added yet another layer of translation to my own renditions in English. I have worked only with the Spanish versions of the poems. As a coda, I include five poems previously unpublished, from her latest book.

Like the experience I had working on Julia Uceda's poetry, this one finds both delight and frustration in translating poems that thrive on difficulty and strangeness. Similarly too, I have tried to retain that strangeness and mystery without sacrificing readability. For this reason, I used the word "longing" for the original "nostalgia" in most cases, because nostalgia in English has other, more limiting connotations that do not express the broader notion Pujol seems to suggest. To take another example: in "First Contemplation," a poem that Biruté Ciplijauskaité considers worthy of inclusion in any anthology (2000, 447), the phrase in line one, "El tiempo no se sucede," is both transparent and complex. I could have expressed it as "Time does not pass (or happen)," since the verb *suceder* means "to happen" but also "to succeed" or "to follow"; and *sucederse*, "to follow one another." Time happens, it passes, but does not normally "follow." Pujol has not written "el tiempo pasa," however, but "se sucede," so I decided to render it as "Time does not follow," partly because in the penultimate line, she says: "Time does not follow. I leave myself and go to this." The verbs—follow *versus*

19

leave and go—seemed to play off each other. But ultimately, I stayed with "Time does not follow," because it sounded somewhat strange in English and that is what I wanted to retain of Sara Pujol's poetry.

My deepest thanks to Julia Uceda, Carol Maier especially, Alane Rollings, and Bob Fedorchek for their advice and suggestions, and to Sara Pujol Russell for writing this poetry.

Selected Bibliography

Sara Pujol Russell

Poetry

Inquietud de pleniluni. 1980. (Recull Prize)

Omega d'amor. In Grup l'Espiadimonis: *Tramada*. Tarragona: Institut d'Estudis Tarraconenses Ramon Berenguer IV (Diputació de Tarragona), 1980.

Mar maduixa. In *6 Poetes 83*. Barcelona: Associació de Joves Escriptors/Edicions del Mall, Col.lecció Impermeable 3, 1983. (Poesia Amadeu Oller Prize)

Ningú a les voltes de l'aire. In Grup l'Espiadimonis: *Versifonies*. Tarragona: Institut d'Estudis Tarraconenses Ramon Berenguer IV, 1987.

Lentitud d'hivern. In Grup l'Espiadimonis: *Mansardas*. Tarragona: Diputació de Tarragona, 1997.

El fuego tiende su aire / El aire tiende a su fuente. Ferrol: Colección Esquío de Poesía, 1999.

Intacto asombro en la luz del silencio / El silencio del loto, la luz de las rosas. Ferrol: Colección Esquío de Poesía, 2001.

Para decir sí a la carencia, sí a la naranja, al azafrán en el pan / Piel de pan que tiende a lo absoluto. Ferrol: Colección Esquío de Poesía, 2004.

Criticism

Uceda, Julia. *En el viento, hacia el mar, 1959–2002*. Edited by Sara Pujol Russell. Seville: Fundación José Manuel Lara, 2002.

Translations of Her Poetry

Il fuoco del silenzio. I Quaderni di Abanico, 34–35. Translated and edited by Emilio Coco. Bari: Levanti Editori, 2001.

Sentire la carenza. I Quaderni della Valle, 54. Translated and edited by Emilio Coco. Bari: Levanti Editori, 2004.

21

Criticism on Sara Pujol Russell

Camarero, Manuel. Review of *El fuego tiende su aire*. *Voz y Letra* 11, no.2 (2000): 170–73.

Ciplijauskaité, Biruté. *La construcción del yo femenino en la literatura*. Serie 2, no. 9. Cádiz: Publicaciones de la Universidad de Cádiz, 2004. 333–35; 403-05; 408.

———. "Criatura frente a la creación." *Salina* 14 (2000): 159–68.

———. "Desde la marginalidad hacia el centro a través de la palabra." In *Identidades culturales*, edited by María Ángeles Hermosilla Álvarez and Amalia Pulgarín Cuadrado, 211–28. Córdoba: Universidad de Córdoba, 2001.

———. "Los gozos de la contemplación." In *The Discovery of Poetry: Essays in Honor of Andrew P. Debicki*, edited by Roberta Johnson, 155–71. Boulder, CO: Society of Spanish and Spanish-American Studies, 2003.

———. "Intemporal, sin fecha, desde siempre volabas." *VII Encuentro de mujeres poetas*, 92–105. Granada: Universidad de Granada, 2003.

———. Review of *El fuego tiende su aire*. *World Literature Today* 74, no.2 (Spring 2000): 447.

Gezzi, Massimo. Review of *Il fuoco del silenzio*. *Pagine,* no. 34 (January–April 2002): 29.

Mantero, Manuel. "Carta a Sara Pujol." In *El fuego tiende su aire / El aire tiende a su fuente*, by Sara Pujol Russell, 115–18. Ferrol: Colección Esquío de Poesía, 1999.

Navarro Durán, Rosa. Review of *Intacto asombro en la luz del silencio*. *Anthropos* 195 (2002): 193–96.

Peñas-Bermejo, Francisco J. "Intimidad y trascendencia en la poesía de Sara Pujol." *Cuadernos de ALDEEU* 20, no. 1 (2004): 102–11.

Sans, Sara. "Sara Pujol. Poeta." *La Vanguardia*, July 22, 1999: 2.

Uceda, Julia. "Antiprólogo." In *El fuego tiende su aire / El aire tiende a su fuente*, by Sara Pujol Russell, 9–11. Ferrol: Colección Esquío de Poesía, 1999.

———. "Aproximaciones a la poesía de Sara Pujol." *Ínsula,* no. 683 (November 2003): 23, 25–26.

Valcárcel, Xulio. "El fuego tiende su aire." *El Ideal Gallego*, November 7, 1999, 4.

Valis, Noël. Review of *Intacto asombro en la luz del silencio*. *Letras Femeninas* 28, no. 2 (December 2002): 197.

Villagrasa, Enrique. Review of *El fuego tiende su aire*. *Diari de Tarragona*, July 3, 1999, 50. Also in *Ficciones. Revista de Letras,* Fall 1999/Winter 2000, 14.

The Poetry
of Sara Pujol Russell

From: *El fuego tiende su aire* (*Fire Floats its Air*)

Contemplación primera

Amanece febrero. Mediodía. El tiempo no se sucede.
Qué belleza el agua y la tregua que así se contemplan y callan,
el aire que suave me respira y a mí sabe, y sabe de mí
y me roba el alma para entregármela después transparente
y feliz. El aire me conduce ligera por los campos de heno
de mi corazón, ahora tranquilos, liberados, llenos
de esta savia nueva y esta fuerza indulgente que me colma.
Inmovilidad ante el mundo. Inmovilidad del mundo
que, suave y silencioso, me encauza hacia mí misma
y vuelo amorosamente sobre lo que ha sido y lo que será.
Qué feliz lejos de todo, todo lejos: el verano,
las regiones saladas, el tiempo, la distancia, la vida.
La palabra es la mirada. Con sorpresa, levanto los ojos
y contemplo con emoción que el mar me mira. ¡Felicidad!
Y también las palmeras, la arena de azafrán y aquel antiguo
olivo tuyo. ¡Oh, Señor! La música me asombra. Me escucha.
Por primera vez, estoy en ellos y ellos en mí. Mi corazón
henchido de mi alma y mi alma henchida de mi corazón.
¡Armonía buscada siempre fuera cuando estabas tan cerca!
¡Ceguera de la donación que nos ciega y ciega a los otros
y más nos hiere y nos deja con la vida contra la vida!
Mediodía. El tiempo no se sucede. Salgo de mí y voy a él
y a él me debo. Por fin, la unión deseada me ha sido concedida.

First Contemplation

February dawns. Midday. Time does not follow.
This is silent beauty: truce and water are mirrors of contemplation.
The silk of air is my breath and taste,
air knows and steals my soul, then gives it back transparent.
Content. Air leads lightly through hayfields
of the heart, tranquil now, free and filled
with new sap, this forgiving force overflowing me.
Immobility before the world. Immobility of the world,
soft and silent, rivers toward me
as I soar with love over what was and what will be.
How sweet to be far from everything, everything far: summer,
regions of salt, time, distance, life.
Words see. Surprised, I raise my eyes
and contemplate, such joy!, the sea looking at me.
And too: palm trees, saffron sands, that ancient
olive tree of yours. Oh, Lord! Music astonishes, listens to me.
I am in them and they in me for the first time. Heart
brims with soul, soul brims with heart.
Harmony was always somewhere else yet you were right here!
Blindness of a gift that blinds us all:
the more it wounds leaves us life against life.
Midday. Time does not follow. I leave myself and go to this.
I owe myself this. Desired, granted at last: this oneness.

Tiempo de luz, tiempo de agua

Luz. ¡Tanta luz y agua! El agua de una fuente que no existe
—existe sólo en mí—mana incesante sobre la luz,
sobre el agua clara y triste que imagino y que me inunda.
Viene hacia mí y yo voy hacia ella, y juntas
¿dónde vamos? Ella nace del tiempo y yo soy el tiempo.
Por un instante, quiero ser ella y sentirme deslizar,
sin angustia, hacia un lago verde y azul y muy sonoro.
No, no es el mar ni es el río lo que deseo,
sino este saberse límite sin nostalgia,
sin esperar nada, serenidad, sin esperar nada más
que la noche y después el alba y después, de nuevo, la noche.
Ella nace del tiempo y vive con el tiempo, ¡oh, feliz!,
y yo sólo soy tiempo que toma mi cuerpo para existir.
Toma mi forma, mi aire y mi carne dichosa, y me deja
desnuda de todo ante el alba, desnuda el alma ante el mar,
ante la vida desnuda y, desnuda de mí, pienso,
siento. Siento el agua de la fuente manando y me siento
—¡oh, corazón, ajeno a ti mismo!—un poco, un poco más lejos.
Luz de agua, agua de luz, río y mar, ¡deteneos!
Y dejadme ser tiempo sin carencia,
ser hospedaje, estancia o aljibe para mi cuerpo,
ser lago, dulce y leve lago, de palabra y silencio.

Time of Light, Time of Water

Light. So much light and water! Water of a fountain that is not
—only in me—flows in a stream over light,
over the image of clear, sad water like a flood inside.
It moves toward me, I toward it, where do we go
together? It is born of time and I am time.
In one instant, I want to be water, without pain,
sliding into green echoes in a blue lake.
It's not the sea, not the river I want,
but to know one's limits, not longing,
expecting nothing, to be serene, expecting nothing
but night, then dawn and after that, night again.
It is born of time and lives in time, content!
I am only time taking my body in order to exist.
It takes my form, my air, my sweet flesh. I am left
totally stripped before the dawn, my soul stripped before the sea,
before life stripped and, stripped of myself, I can think,
feel. And sense the flow of the fountain's water. I am
—this alien heart—a little, a little more distance.
The light of water, the water of light, river and sea, stop!
Let me be time completely,
let me be refuge, a room, a well for my body,
a lake, fragrant and light, of word and silence.

La noche me llama sereno aire, sereno sueño

Noche. Oscura noche. Serenidad. Nada me turba. Serenidad.
El aire me acompaña silente por suaves caminos de la noche,
y la noche me llama por mi nombre de esposa y le soy fiel.
Sí, le soy fiel como el color es fiel a la luz y el blanco al negro,
como es fiel la hierba a su río, el río al mar, y el sueño a su sueño.
Me entrego, amante, a su cuerpo infinito para sentirme cuerpo,
para sentirme noche en la noche serena, y oír mi nombre.
Me entrego, ligera, a mi cuerpo para saber que soy, que existo,
que todavía me hiere la clara belleza de las rosas,
y el mar y el intenso olor a niebla y las vides rojas
y el verso y la palabra dicha, y la palabra oculta.
Sí, me hiere constante, intensamente, lo bello en la belleza.
Me entrego, herida de belleza, a mi cuerpo ardiente y temporal
para reunirme, al fin feliz, con la sabiduría del alma.
Su canto, que todo lo comprende porque todo lo ha vivido,
me sosiega en roja selva, en agua clara, en complacido abrazo
que une el horizonte y la piedra, el árbol y la sombra,
el miedo a la vida y la dorada fuerza del fruto.
Olor, cálido olor a nostalgia hoy perdida sin nostalgia.
Ya nada me turba. La noche me acompaña suave por mis caminos.
Mi nombre me llama y nada respondo. Soy aire y sueño silencioso.

Night Calls Me Serene Air, Serene Sleep

Night. Dark night. Serenity. Nothing disturbs me. Serenity.
Air is my silent companion on the silk roads of night,
and night calls me by my name of wife and I am faithful.
Yes, I am faithful as color is faithful to light and white to black,
as grass is faithful to river, river to sea, and dream to the dream.
I give myself, with love, to its infinite body. I am this body,
I am this night in serene night. I hear my name.
I give myself, lightly, to my body and know that I am, I exist.
The transparent beauty in roses still wounds me,
the sea wounds me, the intense smell of fog, enflamed vines
and poetry, the spoken word and the hidden word.
What is beautiful in beauty wounds me constantly, intensely.
I surrender, beauty's wound, to my burning body of time
which flows, happy at last, into the knowing soul.
Soul's song perceiving everything, lives everything,
holds me in the grace of red trees, clear water, in the embrace
entwining horizon with stone, tree with shadow,
fear of life with the golden force of fruit.
Odor, the warm odor of longing so lost it misses longing itself.
Now nothing bothers me. Night like silk goes with me on my walks.
My name calls and I say nothing. I am air and silent sleep.

Origen del verbo, germinación de la tierra

¡Oh, dulce azar, que eliges, sin voluntad ni capricho, la hora
de nuestra tristeza y el justo momento de nuestra alegría!
¿Cómo puede la idea seducir al sentimiento y no saberlo?
¿Cómo puede desfallecer todo sentimiento sin prever horas
ni años, dando la vida, perdiéndola, sin cesar jamás?
Con un grito, alzo el puñal con que me habéis quebrantado el alma,
danza de luz: caigo de rodillas y esculpo en la tierra un llanto
intenso, poderoso y necesario para volver a la vida.
Me recogió una tarde de invierno crecida en primavera:
desde entonces, la palabra me acecha y yo aguardo sus signos.

Origin of the Word, Flowering of the Earth

Sweet chance, it is yours to choose—there's no caprice, no control—
the hour of our unhappiness, the perfect moment of our joy!
Can thought seduce emotion and not know it?
Can emotion fade away and not predict the hours,
the years giving life, losing it, with no relief in sight?
With a cry, I raise the knife with which you broke my soul,
a dance of light: I fall on my knees and sculpt in the earth a weeping
so intense, so powerful and necessary that I return to life.
A winter afternoon heavy with spring seized me:
since then, the word stalks me and I await its signs.

Con las manos sobre la ausencia

Llegará la noche y pensaré en qué he pasado el día.
Sólo he contemplado. Me ha vivido el azul del alba
y el claro sol de la tarde. Y nada más. Enamorada
y celosa de su mansedumbre, nada turba la calma.
Me he sentado, con los ojos cerrados, con las manos sobre
la ausencia, y he sentido el ligero y suave pasar del tiempo
sobre la piel, su fluir lento y preciso en torno al corazón.
El no piensa ni siente y, en su quietud, permanece prendido
en todo lo que siente en su nombre, en todo lo que tiembla
con anhelo deseando su quietud. El tiempo no pasa,
sólo fluye. Carente de vida propia y de angustia ausente
da vida, sin desvelo, al mar, al sol, al alba y a la noche.
Su quietud nos vuelve indefensos y débiles y extraños.
Su quietud es nuestra inquietud y nuestra melancolía.

With my Hands upon Absence

Night will come and I will think on how I've spent the day.
In meditation. Azure dawn gave breath to me
and the clear sun of afternoon. Nothing more. Nothing
disturbs the brooding calm, in love with its own tenderness.
I sit down, eyes closed, with my hands upon
absence, and sense the soft, light passing of time
over my skin, its slow, precise flow through the heart.
It does not think or feel and, in the silence, is caught
in everything the name senses, in everything that trembles
with longing, desiring that quiet. Time passes not,
only flows. Bereft itself of life, absent of anguish,
giving careless life to the sea, to sun, dawn and night.
This quiet renders us helpless, weak and strange.
This quiet is our nerves and our despair.

Aroma de mirra, aroma de soledad

No hay melancolía más triste que el humo negro y perfumado
de la mirra quemando sueños y naranjos que nunca fueron;
que el humo negro de la mirra quebrando ágil lo que hemos sido,
lo que jamás seremos, lo que nunca amamos creyendo amar.
Aroma de soledad en viernes, en el aire, en el invierno
que arde más allá, mucho más allá, de su querer y su olvido,
que arde en un vaso, en unos ojos en aromada soledad
—unos ojos que han visto tantos fuegos que son cristal en llama—,
y arde sin saber que una mirada transforma la nada en tiempo,
la nada en manos abrazadas a las hojas, el todo en nada.
Cántaros sonoros de vino, hombro desnudo, ceguera oscura,
estoy con vosotros como si fuera invierno y humo de mirra.
Herida estoy de eternidad, de tiempo en el centro de la herida.
Sin melancolía estoy. Viví siempre con la melancolía,
de la melancolía, de la nostalgia, con la nostalgia a hombros.
Hoy, sin más, las he dejado partir de mi vida sin esfuerzo,
o, quizás, es tanta la nostalgia que ya no sé qué es nostalgia.
¡Loca pasión del ser, ser y ser en todo y en todo momento!
No hay nada más triste que el humo blanco de una tarde en invierno.

The Smell of Myrrh, the Smell of Solitude

There is nothing more melancholy than the black, perfumed smoke
of myrrh burning dreams and orange trees that never existed;
than the quick black smoke of myrrh breaking what we were,
what we will never be, what we never loved believing it was love.
The smell of solitude on Friday, in the air, in the winter
that burns beyond, beyond desire and far forgetting,
burning in glass, burning in the eyes of perfumed solitude
—eyes that saw the fires of enflamed crystal—
burning and not knowing one glance transforms nothingness into time,
nothingness into hands clutching leaves, everything into nothing.
Cups sing with wine, a bare shoulder, dark blindness,
I am with you as if it were winter and the fumes of myrrh.
I am wounded with eternity, with time in the heart of my wound.
I am not melancholy. I have always lived with melancholy,
in melancholy, in longing, with the burden of nostalgia.
Today, just like that, I let them slip out of my life,
or maybe, there is so much longing I do not know what longing is.
The madness of passion to be, to be, to be in every thing, in every moment!
There is nothing sadder than the white smoke of a winter afternoon.

Mi desnudez es olor a sueños

Nostalgia, despeñadero de marfil, recia aljaba de sueños,
brocada noche del pasado, brocal ardiente del futuro,
corazón batiendo el aire, el agua, la tierra, la sangre a remos,
sentido de permanencia, soledad en los cinco sentidos:
cuando todo es nostalgia se vive ya sin nostalgia por nada,
vives ya desnudo, roto en brasa, abierto sólo a la fragancia.
A veces, querrías sentir nostalgia, una nostalgia de alberca
por una ausencia, un niño hecho árbol en flor, un dolor hecho mar,
por un río, una caricia en aljófar de luna . . . y no la sientes.
Mi nostalgia es entusiasmo, es nostalgia de forma en movimiento,
es la nostalgia sensual de la abundancia, la alegría, el gozo
y el deseo. Nostalgia pura que no se rinde al sol del tiempo.
Nostalgia por la belleza, la lluvia que es lluvia por su nombre,
que es belleza porque vive ajena a mi mirar atribulado,
a mi callar vencido, a mis vencidas manos en su alto fuego.
No es desolación lo que siento, sino una rara necesidad
de medida: por un momento, quisiera que lo infinito fuera
finito y tangible, que lo finito fuera infinito por siempre;
por un momento, necesito bañarme en todas las fuentes y aguas
llenas de estrellas y horizontes y horas de oro, verdes y redondas
—no, no, no en la sal del mar, que ya conozco y me mata en muerta flor
a la deriva—; beber todas las lluvias que me dejarán ser
río entre los ríos y racimos de hielo y niebla entre los bosques;
probar el sabor del cielo al alba, cada anochecer, en la noche,
y saber si lo azul es dulce o amargo, si lo negro o la luna
tienen sabor a tristeza o a retazos de nieve en alegría.
Necesito ser amor en el amor y, como el amor que nunca
tiende al pasado o la rosa que nunca contempla fugacidad,
vivir todos los amores y en un solo cuerpo prender su esencia:
(amor, origen y curso del amor: cogida mortal en la arena)
¡un amor infinito en mi corazón sembrado de finitud!
Nostalgia, despeñadero de luna, ardiente aljaba en muchas noches,
abierta estoy en desnudez, en brasas, con un solo olor a sueños.

My Being Naked is the Smell of Dreams

Longing is an ivory precipice, a thick quiver of dreams,
the past's brocaded night, the future's burning mouth,
the heart beating like oars against air, water, earth, blood,
the sense of permanence, solitude in the five senses:
when everything is longing you end up longing nothing,
you live naked, broken on the rack, open only to the fragrant trace.
Sometimes, you would like to feel longing, the deep well of longing
for an absence, for a child who is the flowering tree, a pain which is the sea,
for a river, a caress in the pearl drop of the moon . . . but you do not feel it.
My longing's enthusiasm, longing for the moving form,
the sensual longing for abundance, joy, delight
and desire. Pure longing that will not yield to the sun of time.
Longing for beauty, for rain that is rain because of its name,
that is beauty for living apart from my troubled gaze,
from my defeated silence, from my defeated hands thrust in the flames.
It is not desolation I feel, but a rare need
for measure: for a moment, I wish the infinite were
finite and tangible, that the finite were infinite forever;
for a moment, I need to bathe in all the fountains and waters
full of stars, horizons and the green circles of golden hours
—not in the salt of the sea I know condemns the flower to drifting
death. I need to drink rain and more rain, to be
a river among rivers and clusters of ice and fog in the woods;
to taste the dawn sky at dusk, every night,
to know if blue is sweet or bitter, if black or the moon
tastes like something sad or shines like scraps of snow.
I need to be love in love, love that never
stretches to the past, the rose that never contemplates the fleeting.
I need to live every love and capture its essence in a single body:
(love, origin and the course of love: fatally gored in the sand)
An infinite love in my heart seeded with the finite!
Longing, precipice of the moon, burning quiver night after night,
I am open nakedness, bright coals, with a single smell of dreams.

Vivir en palabra callada

Estoy bien, aquí, en minuciosa soledad, sin más compañía
que mi propia palabra. Me asedia, me extraña, me sorprende,
me cautiva, me habla, me escucha, y yo deseo interpretarla
como ella me interpreta. Sabe de mí más que yo misma.
Le pregunto por mí y, bondadosa, me besa y me sosiega.
Quiero explicarle tantas cosas que sólo ella entenderá . . .
Con suavidad, me abraza y con un gesto me indica el futuro.
Conozco el mundo a través de ti y a través de ti lo vivo.
Vivo si tú me das vida, me salvo si me ofreces salvación.
Aquí me llega la abierta fragancia de las rosas de antaño
y tú, en silencio, me traes ramos de hierba, y un cesto lleno
de flores rojas y blancas y amarillas. Una cerrada hoguera
de aromas y color me enseña el camino que tú quieres que siga.

To Live in the Silent Word

I am fine here, teeming with solitude, and no more company
than my own word tracking me. She misses and surprises me,
captivates, speaks and listens to me. I yearn to interpret her
as she interprets me. She knows more of me than I do myself.
If I ask about myself, she gives me kisses and comforts me with kindness.
I want to explain so many things that only she will understand.
Softly she embraces me and with a sign shows the future.
I know the world through you and through you I live it.
I live when you give me life, I am saved when you save me.
An open fragrance of antique roses comes to me here.
Silent, you bring me handfuls of grass and a basket
filled with flowers, red, white and yellow. A sealed fire storm
of scents and colors to show the path you want me to follow.

Como ciervo que bebe el silencio de la rosa

Noche. Mucha noche. ¡Cuánta noche para mí y mi solo cuerpo!
Demasiada para no velar tanto recuerdo y tanto olvido.
Cuánto amor, y qué grande y qué breve, para una sola vida.
¡Tanto amor y desamor para un cuerpo y una sola vida!
Cuánto mundo para unos ojos tan pequeños y tan abstractos,
tan concretos, fragmentarios, como el querer de un árbol en su hoja.
Cuántos cuerpos vividos, por vivir, para conocer la dimensión
del mundo y no alcanzar nunca la profundidad del tacto, de la llama.
Cuánta tristeza y felicidad, como el tiempo sobre este tiempo,
como el ciervo que va a la fuente y bebe el silencio de la rosa.
Cuántos sueños por vivir sin medida en el umbral de locura
y pureza, en el umbral de acacias que el mar oculta y detiene.
Cuántas palabras ya dichas para sentirnos todavía inocentes.
Cuánta voz escrita en piedra por temor a perder la voz en el aire.
Cuánta infancia junta, cuánta juventud junta en tan poco tiempo,
para poder ser libres de nosotros y dejar de ser libres.
Noche. Qué poca noche para velar tu cuerpo y tu sueño.
¿Cómo huir ya del recuerdo y de la celosía del alba?

Like a Deer Drinking the Silence of the Rose

Night. Night upon night. All this night for me and my one body!
Too much not to brood over so much memory and forgetting.
So much love, vast yet so brief, for only one life.
So much love and hate for a body and only one life!
So much world for eyes so small and abstract,
so concrete, yet fragmentary, like the leafy desire of a tree.
So many bodies lived in, still to live, to know the dimension
of the world but never to reach the depths of touch, of flame.
So much misery and delight, like time heaped upon time,
like the deer that goes to the fountain and drinks the silence of the rose.
So many unmeasured dreams left to live on the threshold of madness
and purity, on the threshold of acacias the sea hides and holds back.
So many words are spoken just to feel innocent.
So many voices written in stone fear the voice lost in the air.
So many childhoods, youths, in so little time,
just to be free of ourselves and stop being free.
Night. So little night to watch over your body and your sleep.
How to escape from memory, from the latticed jealousy of daybreak?

Creación de mi nombre

Si la aurora surgió del caos. Si la luz, de la oscuridad.
Si la palabra emergió de la ceguera y las nubes del vino.
Si la belleza brotó de la clara conciencia de la muerte,
y la verdad se alimentó de ella y, así, también el amor,
mi corazón nació una noche de azabache enamorada.
Mi cuerpo, un mediodía de invierno celoso de la noche.
Mi tiempo, en un jardín de rosas donde habitaban los sueños.
Mi aliento, en la baja niebla, en los labios de un bosque encendido.

Creation of my Name

What if dawn streamed from chaos and light from darkness.
What if the word emerged from blindness and clouds from wine.
What if beauty grew from the clear conscience of death,
truth fed off it, and so too love,
my heart was born one jet-black, enamored night.
My body, one midday in winter jealous of the night.
My time, in a garden of roses where dreams lived.
My breath, in the deep-down fog, in the lips of a burning woods.

Soledad de piedra

Mi lago es de piedra y de luna. La memoria es roja piedra.
La luna es la distancia entre labio y sueño, entre sueño y valle.
Fuera, coro en juego de los niños, siempre hijos de los otros,
hijos a quienes nunca llamarás hijos ni verde luna.
Canta el ave en su jaula, prisionera de rejas y claveles.
Prisionera del aire y la sangre, canto contra soledad.
Soledad, soledad que nos haces leves, diestros con la sombra,
alegres cuando vemos que te alejas alegre hacia las águilas,
no te prometo fidelidad, ni compañía ni alimento.
Mi camino es el amor. Con todo, tu estancia, hoy, me es venturosa.
No, no renuncio a ti si detrás del clavel me espera el esposo,
si al escribir mi verso te inclinas suave y besas con tu fuego
la nieve de mi frente, si acaricias la noche en mi ribera,
si, azul, me recuerdas que tengo recuerdos que son como el trigo,
si me recuerdas que es necesario este pozo de piedra y luna.

Solitude of Stone

My lake is stone and moon. Memory is red stone.
The moon is the distance between lips and sleep, between sleep and valley.
Outside, a chorus of children at play, always other people's children,
children you will never call your own, never call green moon.
The bird sings in its cage, a prisoner of iron bars and carnations.
Prisoner of the air and blood, I sing in the face of solitude.
Solitude, solitude, you make us light: experts of shadows,
happy to see you move away happy, toward the eagles.
I cannot promise you fidelity, company or sustenance.
My way is love. Even so, your visit is lucky for me today.
No, I will not give you up if the carnation hides a husband-in-waiting,
if I write my poetry and you lean over softly with your fire and kiss
my face of snow, if you caress my night shore,
if the color blue reminds me I have memories like the wheat,
if you remind me this well of stone and moon is necessary.

Soledad de luna

Soledad, déjame sola con la palabra contra la palabra
hecha verso, con el tacto a flor de noche, a flor de flor, de ti.
Luna llena, blanca, sobre los tejados de pizarra negra,
la luna blanca sobre el negro cuervo, un cuervo blanco de luna,
sobre el río blanco y la piedra blanca a la luz de la luna,
sobre la campana de luna que toca a medianoche, a sueños.
Creo que no pienso. Que no pienso en nada tangible. Es como
si el trigo, el río, la piedra o la luna estuviesen en mí
y no los pudiera pensar. ¡Maravilla! Las dimensiones
de mi cuerpo son, por un momento y lugar, las de mi espíritu.
Paz. Entrego mi felicidad al pecho abierto que la quiera.
Canta, de nuevo, la campana. Es medianoche en mi cuerpo, en mi aliento.

Solitude of Moon

Solitude, leave me alone with words pressed against each other,
into poetry, brushing the night, brushing the flower, you.
Full white moon on black slate roofs,
white moon on black crow, a crow white with the moon,
on the white river and the white stone in moonlight,
on the moon-bell that rings at midnight, in dreams.
I do not believe I am thinking. Not of anything tangible. It is as if
wheat, river, stone and moon were within me
so I could not think them. Amazing! The dimensions
of my body are, for one moment and place, those of my spirit.
Peace. I surrender my happiness to the ample heart that wants it.
The bell sings again. It is midnight in my body, in my breath.

Interpretación de la rosa

Cogí la rosa y sus pétalos fueron naves de naufragio.
Cada pétalo, errático, era tiempo que no podía detener
ni con los ojos ni con el corazón ni con las manos llenas,
y fui tiempo, nómada tiempo, para siempre. Fui, soy, ofrenda
de abundancia enalteciendo la llama del aire. Soy la blanca
novia del tiempo que espera ausente ser blanca esposa de la vida.
Te ofrezco mis bienes, duración y brevedad, si me das,
generoso, brevedad y duración y aire blanco y otra rosa,
y otra. Paso abril reuniendo naves y pétalos, y todo
se confunde: la sangre y la savia, la lluvia y la sangre, la sangre
y las flores, la memoria y la razón, la ilusión y la locura.
¿Cómo separarlo? ¿Cómo devolverte todo lo que te robé
una noche de amor? ¿Cómo devolverme todo lo que me he robado,
todo cuanto he velado en la noche y no era ni justo ni necesario?
¿Cómo vivir con el corazón en la rosa y no ser tiempo vencido?
Errática, te pido que me sujetes a la flor del eucalipto,
a la carne del lirio, a la furia de las aves, al mar en calma;
que me sujetes, con tu fuerza, a mi furia y a mi calma de abril.

Interpretation of the Rose

I picked the rose and the petals were shipwrecked vessels.
Each drifting petal was time I could not stop
not with my eyes, not with my heart, not with my full hands.
I was time, nomadic time, forever. I was, I am, an offering
of riches exalting the air in flames. I am the white
bride of time absently waiting to be the white bride of life.
I offer you my earthly goods, duration and brevity, if you are generous
and give me brevity and duration, white air, another rose,
and another. I spend April joining ships and petals and everything
is mixed together: blood and sap, rain and blood, blood
and flowers, memory and reason, illusion and madness.
How can I separate all this? How can I return everything I stole from you
one night of love? How can I return everything I stole from myself,
everything I brooded over at night, what a stupid waste of time?
How can I live with the heart in the rose? Not be defeated by time?
Drifting away, I ask you to bind me to the eucalyptus flower,
to the flesh of the iris, to the fury of birds, to the stilled sea.
I ask you to bind me, with all your strength, to my fury, to my April calm.

Angustia sosegada

Esta tarde escribo para alejarme de mí, para ahuyentar
de mí el delirio, la locura del labio que tiembla en la rosa,
para apartar de mí la primavera y batir la lumbre en dulce
apartamiento. Todo me es ajeno y todo es común espejo.
La distancia y la proximidad son alas de la misma luna.
Amor y desamor son, ahora, noche de la misma llama.
Sé que todo lo que une, separa. Que todo lo que separa,
al mismo tiempo, une. Y sé que, así, pasamos la vida, uniendo
y dividiendo la vida, uniendo el grano y derramando la siembra.
Imposible es evitarlo. Imposible requerir y encontrar
la proporción. El amor nos separa de nosotros mismos
para entregarnos, indolentes, al alba. El alba se separa
de nosotros para devolvernos, ungidos, al desamor.
El desamor nos separa de los labios y nos convierte
en rosaleda que crece junto a la lluvia, junto a la voz,
junto a la calle, junto a la nada que crece ebria entre la nada.
Si adelanto un paso, dejo atrás el mar y siento su peso
de hiedra en la espalda, el peso del cielo en la frente y, en los ojos,
brasa de espigas, y no puedo andar, y no puedo mirar,
y no puedo, ya, recordar. No recuerdo y niego el olvido.

The Comfort of Anguish

This afternoon I write to get away from myself, to drive away
my delirium, the madness of lips trembling on the rose,
to separate the spring from me, to beat the fire into soft
seclusion. Everything is alien to me and everything is the same mirror.
Distance and proximity are the wings of the same moon.
Love and hate are now the night of the same flame.
I know everything that unites, separates. Everything that separates,
at the same time unites. Knowing we spend life, uniting
and dividing life, uniting the grain and spilling the seed.
Impossible to avoid it. Impossible to demand, to find
proportion. Love separates us
handing us over, indolent, to the dawn. Dawn separates
to return us, anointed, to hate.
Hate separates our lips and converts us
into a rose garden that grows beside the rain, beside the voice,
beside the street, beside nothingness growing drunkenly amid nothing.
If I take a step forward, I leave behind the sea and feel its weight
of ivy on my back, the weight of the sky on my face and, in my eyes,
coal-bright ears of grain, and I cannot walk and I cannot look,
I no longer remember. I do not remember and I deny forgetting.

Oración al atardecer

Me divido en cuerpo y alba, en mar y cielo, en sol y amor,
para ser rosa en la honda que busca el acorde del aire:
y quedo dividida en primavera y otoño, norte y sur,
en soledad tejida de fragmentos, tejida de invierno.
He dividido el sendero en ríos para evitar el paso de la angustia.
He fragmentado el ansia, la sed, la fe y el sueño para poder soñar.
He abierto la roja manzana, como quien abre el mar en alas y tierra,
para saber del bien y del mal, saber qué es la tentación
y cómo es la virtud. He fragmentado la brasa que nos abrasa
para hacer del fuego, del fuego nuestro, fuego en sobria unidad.
Me vence el alma este solo caminar solitario en soledad. Me vence.
Venzo el camino si me alejo de mí y voy, fuera de mí, hacia ti:
vivo en tus labios y en ellos me encuentro, me comprendo,
    me levanto.
Escribo desde los labios, desde el beso que acierta la palabra,
la palabra justa si la tomo de tus labios en el beso.
Y desde tus labios, contemplo. Y sólo desde tus labios, ruego.
Ruego que el poema me dé lo que la vida me ha robado.
Que la tristeza me dé lo que la felicidad no ha podido.
Que la felicidad me dé lo que la tristeza me ha negado.

A Prayer at Dusk

I divide into body and daybreak, into sea and sky, into sun and love,
to be a rose in the slingshot marking a chord in the air:
and I remain divided into spring and fall, north and south,
into solitude woven of fragments, woven of winter.
I divided the path into rivers to avoid the passage of grief.
I fragmented anxiety, thirst, faith and sleep to be able to dream.
I split open the red apple, as you open the sea into wings and earth,
to know good and evil, to know what temptation is
and what virtue is. I fragmented the fiery coals that burn us,
to make of the fire, our fire, a taut fire of unity.
This simple walking alone in solitude defeats my soul. It defeats me.
I defeat the road if I leave myself and go outside, toward you:
I live in your lips and in them I find myself, I understand myself,
    I lift myself up.
I write from the lips, from the kiss won by the word,
the precise word if I take it in the kiss from your lips.
And from your lips, I contemplate. And only from your lips, I pray.
I pray that the poem give me what life stole.
That sadness give me what happiness could not.
That happiness give me what sadness denied.

Tú, caminante

Tú, caminante, que llegas lleno de grave invierno y de luz
a esta primavera—un invierno que es de todos, una luz
que para ti sólo has creado—, sonríe, no te preguntes,
no preguntes lo que ya no tiene respuesta, no te detengas
a beber del tiempo pasado, del paso errante del amor.
No detengas la edad por una falsa sonrisa, no detengas
los jazmines por una respuesta incierta. No te detengas
a esperar el verano. El solo vendrá a buscarte. Mayo está
en la noche antes de ser noche de mayo. El estío yace
dormido en tu sangre y sólo ella le dará su rojo ardiente.
Abandona el invierno y la luz en la hiedra y, ahora, sé
sólo primavera. Y cuando llegue la noche, bella y fragante,
no salgas a la noche a escuchar su canto y su aroma, no salgas
de la noche y sé tú su canto, su secreto más claro y bello,
el más esperado. No despiertes su brisa. No la apremies
con tu apremio, con tu obstinada tristeza de caminante.
Ella es camino, igual que la primavera, igual que la sonrisa,
y ser camino es ser quietud sin fatiga, ser paz
    sin ribera,
ser bosque sin claveles, ser mar sin agua, ser fruto
    sin ramas.
Sé tú, también, camino y olvida los senderos por donde
has venido. ¿Qué importan? Ya no existen.
    Sólo son tu recuerdo,
tus pies, tu sed. Y ¿qué importa la sed si dentro de la noche,
detrás del labio no corre la sed? ¿Qué importan los pies
si más allá de la noche pierde la vida la muerte?
¿Qué importa el recuerdo si imploras olvido para recordar?
No te detengas a esperar el alba. Ella te sorprenderá.
Únete a ella, hazla tuya, y que ella sea alba del alba en la noche,
que sea su secreto más claro y bello, el menos esperado.
No la despiertes. No la asustes con tu miedo que el aire
sostiene. No la abandones por la rosa, la luz, o por el sueño.
Tú, que llegas lleno de sueños y primavera a esta primavera,
sonríe, no intentes detener la belleza de la tarde,
y pregunta, silencioso, cómo encontrar, cómo llegar
al camino de la noche, cómo nombrarla por su nombre.
Cuando la sientas cuerpo de tu cuerpo, no te asustes. Serás
bosque, quietud sin claveles, mar sin ramas, paz
    sin fatiga.

You, Traveler

You, traveler, arriving full of grave winter and light
to this spring—a winter for everyone, a light
created for you alone—smile, do not ask
what no longer has an answer, do not stop
to drink the past, the errant passage of love.
Do not stop age for a false smile, or
jasmine for an uncertain response. Do not stop
to wait for summer. It will come on its own to look for you. May is
in the night before the night is in May. Summer lies
asleep in your blood and only blood will make it burn red.
Let winter go, light in the ivy, you be
spring alone. And when night comes, lovely and fragrant,
do not listen to the song and scent of night, but stay
in night, you be the song, its clearest, loveliest secret,
the one most expected. Do not wake its breeze. Do not rush it,
rush it, with your obstinate traveler's sadness.
Night is a road, just like the spring, like a smile,
and to be a road is to be stillness without weariness, to be peace without
    a shore,
to be trees without carnations, to be the sea without water, to be fruit
    without branches.
You be a road also, forget the paths by which
you have come. What do they matter? They are no longer here.
    Only your memory,
your feet, your thirst. And what does thirst matter if in night,
behind lips, thirst has not happened? What do feet matter
if beyond night death loses life?
What does memory matter if you beg for oblivion in order to remember?
Do not stop to wait for dawn. It will surprise you.
Be one with it, make it yours, let it be the dawn of dawn in night,
its clearest, loveliest secret, the one least expected.
Do not wake or scare it with your fear held
in air. Do not leave it for the rose, the light, the dream.
You come full of dreams and spring to this spring,
smile, do not try to stop the beauty of afternoon.
Ask, like silence, how do I find, how do I reach
the road of the night, how do I call it by name.
When you feel it as the body of your body, do not be afraid. You will be
a forest, stillness without carnations, the sea without branches, peace
    without weariness.

Conocimiento de la primavera

Cae la tarde y la primavera se desgrana, suave y feliz,
sobre la luz. Las primeras rosas son ya agua en el agua clara.
No quiere permanencia ni coger la belleza de su fruto
porque sabe que fluir es necesario y que, fluyendo, somos
deseo y amor. Se reconoce semilla de sí misma,
y detrás de sus flores se espera. Y espera, libre de todo,
beber el vino para dejarnos libre el agua cristalina,
vivir soledad para dejarnos intacto y puro el amor,
comer el duro pan de la memoria innecesaria para
saborear humildad, prudencia, sobriedad y templanza.
Tiro una piedra de luna y arcilla—no sé si la primera—
contra su sabiduría, y su libertad es mi cautiverio.
La espero detrás de mis manos, en los pétalos, en el alma
que, por fin, ha aprendido que fluir tiene nombre de primavera.

Knowing Spring

Afternoon fades and spring, threshed, is soft and happy,
over light. The first roses are already water in clear water.
It does not want permanence, nor to catch the beauty of fruit
knowing that to flow is necessary. Flowing, we are
desire and love. Spring is its own seed,
and behind the flowers waits. And waits, free of everything,
to drink the wine freeing the water like crystals,
to live solitude leaving us love, intact and pure,
to eat the hard bread of memory unnecessary
for savoring humility, wisdom, moderation and restraint.
I throw a stone of moon and clay—is it the first?—
at spring's all-knowing, and the freedom of spring is my cage.
I wait for it behind my hands, in the petals, in the soul
that finally learns: flow has the name of spring.

Si es de noche y te sorprende

Si es de noche y te sorprende en tu lecho de luna la angustia,
no corras hacia la historia, ni busques la palabra en los silos
ni la perfección que deseas como la angustia te desea.
No corras hacia la lluvia. Olvídala como si todavía
tuviera que existir, como si hoy todavía tuvieras
que nacer y tu sangre te extrañara ya como costumbre.
No busques nada, sólo el jardín donde sentarse y la fuente
donde mirar, donde tenderse y yacer celebrando el silencio.
Silencio y arena de mar son lo mismo. La fuente y el mar
son aire, y de aire es tu leve vida y de aire, tu gran amor.
Si es de noche y te sorprende la felicidad, a ti no vayas,
no corras hacia el futuro. En paz, siéntate a su lado y espera.
No mires tu cielo y tu prado, mírala sólo a ella, abrázala
suavemente y canta tenue, sin cesar, que no piense, altiva,
que duermes o que tus ojos no han sabido verla o tus labios,
selva y volcán de angustia, rendirse no quieren a su armonía.
Si es de noche y te sorprende el aire, eres tú quien te sorprende
y la vida. La fuente en su mar, el mar en tu amor te sorprenden.
No huyas del tiempo aventando el olor de la rosa en la belleza.
No corras hacia los demás, no te huyas. Mira al sur
   y llora.

If it's Night and It Surprises You

If it's night and anguish surprises you in your moonstruck room,
do not chase after the story, or look for the word in silos
or the perfection you ache for as anguish aches for you.
Do not chase after rain. Forget it as though it
still had to exist, as though, today, you still
had to be born and the habit of blood already missed you.
Look for nothing, only the garden to sit in and the fountain
to see, stretched out on the ground celebrating silence.
Silence and the sands of the sea are the same. Fountain and sea
are air, and your feather of a life is air, and your great love is air.
If it's night and happiness surprises you, do not go to yourself,
do not chase after the future. Sit down in peace beside her and wait.
Do not stare at your sky, your field, look only at her, embrace her
gently and sing low, non-stop, so she will not take it wrong,
or think you fell asleep or your eyes cannot see her, or your lips,
a dense volcano of anguish, cannot yield to her harmony.
If it's night and air surprises you, surprise yourself
and life. The fountain in its sea, the sea in your love surprise you.
Do not run away from time fanning the scent of the rose in beauty.
Do not chase after other people, do not run away. Look to the south
   and weep.

De aire la vida

Escucha la vida paseando sobre la arena y mírate
en la fuente. El reflejo que en ella ves no es el mar ni el sueño,
sino el aire, el aire que te mueve y te angustia porque es puro
silencio creciente. Silencio de luna, silencio de árbol,
silencio de aire, de ti, de todo. Calla. No te rebeles.
Contémplala abrazando el polen. Hazte silencio y respire
con armonía de fuego tu vida de aire, sólo de aire,
—oh, tristeza—, pero de aire que puede ser pájaro o piedra,
luz o flor, o aire que al aire vigila como la tormenta
a la calma, el lirio al cielo, el agua herida al río del amor.

Out of Air, Life

Listen to life strolling on the sand and see yourself
in the fountain. The reflection you regard is not the sea or a dream,
but air, the air that moves you to anguish because it is pure
silence growing. Silence of the moon, silence of the tree,
silence of air, of you, of everything. Be quiet. Do not resist.
See it embrace the pollen. Be silent and breathe
with the harmony of fire your life of air, only air,
—this sadness—but air that might be a bird or a stone,
light or a flower, or air that monitors air as the storm
does the calm, the iris the sky, wounded water the river of love.

Septiembre

Septiembre corre hacia otras islas. No le detiene su nombre.
No le detiene el asombro, ni negras voces en su orilla.
Muere lo verde en lo amarillo, leve rumor en el aire,
en la tierra sosegada al filo de la hoja en su lumbre.
No le detienen los pájaros ni las fuentes ni los juncos,
no detiene la tarde, esta tarde que es puro azahar soñado.
Contempla la vendimia y, por ella, aprende la melancolía
del hombre. Mira los campos y sabe del cansancio del alma.
Huele el trigo y descubre los sueños y la noche inesperada.
Nos contempla y conoce, absorto, la profundidad de la carne.
Llegó desamado como llega la soledad, y ahora
rompe su herida y huye, en amor, de su nombre hacia su nombre.

September

September runs toward other islands. The name cannot stop it.
Surprise cannot stop it, or black voices on the shore.
Green dies in yellow, a light murmur in the air,
in the earth lulled by the edge of the leaf in fire.
Neither birds nor fountains nor reeds stop it,
the afternoon cannot stop it, this afternoon's pure dream of orange blossoms.
Go to the wine harvest to learn the melancholy
of man. Look at the fields to know the tiredness of the soul.
Smell the wheat to discover dreams and unexpected night.
The depths of flesh look at us, absorbed, and know us.
It arrived unloved the way solitude arrives, and now
it breaks the wound and flees, in love, from name to name.

Enséñame

Enséñame a oler feliz el tiempo en la luna de abril.
Enséñame a rozar lo eterno con mi asombro y el tuyo.
Enséñame a ver la pena con ojos de oscura lejanía.
Enséñame un nuevo sabor del llanto como si fuera flor.
Enséñame a escuchar lo más vivido como si aún tuviera
que vivirse, como si aún pudiera ser felicidad que no daña,
como si aún pudiéramos ser, pudiéramos ser sueño en lo soñado.

Teach me

Teach me to smell time, happy, in the April moon.
Teach me to brush the eternal lightly with my astonishment and yours.
Teach me to see pain with eyes of dark distance.
Teach me a new taste of tears as if it were a flower.
Teach me to hear the fully alive as if it still were
lived, was happiness that does no harm,
as if we could still be a dream in what is dreamed.

Soledad

Soledad, que armoniosa desciendes por el valle, dime
a qué bosque, a qué mar va el olvido, a qué muerte
    va la muerte.
Desciendes por el valle, en todo te detienes y en nada
te reposas. Qué perfecto es tu talle, qué esbeltas tus formas,
qué ágil tu paso, y nadie te contempla en tu exacta medida.
El amor se piensa, el recuerdo se talla, el sueño se teje.
Imposible es pensar la soledad. Es el agua del río
y el río mismo y su orilla. Es alma y cuerpo al mismo tiempo.
Es caricia y llanto, luz y sombra, ave y aire, espada y muerte.
El sentimiento es soledad, los sentidos son su sombra.
Noche, y aquí estás en mí, ante mí, y eres clavel en mi mano
y eres mi mano en mis ojos, y mis ojos en mi voz.
Soledad, eres silencio y te pareces al silencio.
Eres promesa y te asemejas a la noche oscura.
Eres casi piedad y te nombran como a la ira.
Eres tierra y te vemos como a un sueño pasajero.
Soledad, que siempre niegas lo finito y lo infinito,
no dejes que esta noche huya de mis manos, de mis labios
y mi alma. Tiéndete en mí y en mí descansa tu armonía.

Solitude

Solitude, descending the valley in calm, tell me
to what wild wood, to what sea does forgetting go, to what death does
    death go.
You descend the valley, stopping at everything, resting
at nothing. How perfect your figure, how slender your forms,
how quick your step, yet no one sees your precise measure.
Love can be thought, memory carved out, dreams woven.
It is impossible to conceive solitude. It is the water of the river
and the river itself and the shore. It is body and soul at the same time.
It is a caress and tears, light and shadow, bird and air, sword and death.
To feel is solitude, the senses are its shadow.
Night, you are in me here, before me, a carnation in my hand
and you are my hand in my eyes, and my eyes in my voice.
Solitude, you are silence and you seem like silence.
You are a promise and you seem like dark night.
You are nearly pity and you are called anger.
You are earth and we see you like a passing dream.
Solitude, you always deny the finite and the infinite,
stop this night flying from my hands, from my lips
and my soul. Stretch out in me and in me rest your peace.

Sencillez

La sencillez es una celosía abierta de palabras
calladas. Es un gesto como de pluma o flor que no quiere
ser más gesto que el suyo. Es fresco zaguán donde la esperanza
es sonrisa que gana a la vida. Es tierno cuidado. Un campo
de algodón en invierno, una fuente que no espera el arroyo.
La sencillez es celebración del instante que no aguarda
demora. Es el pensamiento dulce que en su amor siempre mira
como si midiera distancias. Es desnudez donde todo
lo inextinguible se reúne. Es toda belleza guardada.
Es la mano o el alma por otra mano de amor herida.
Doliente zarzal que sueña como si contara caricias.
Duerme poco y vela por lo que es pequeño, ligero y frágil.
Toma su paz, levemente, como si no la mereciera.
Detiene la felicidad y sabe su significado.
Acaso nada se muda en sencillez si triste desencanto
no le ha herido. Acaso nada muda sin nostalgia o sin brisa.
Sencillez, si hoy amara de nuevo, de nuevo te amaría.
Dame, ahora, tu espíritu y crece firme en mi firme fuerza.
Sencillez es decir tu amado nombre que es como la lluvia.

Simplicity

Simplicity is a shutter opened with silent
words. It is a sign of feather or flower that wants
only to be its own sign. It is a cool vestibule where hope
is a smile that wins over life. It is tender care. A field
of cotton in winter, a fountain that does not expect the stream.
Simplicity is celebration of the instant that brooks no
delay. It is sweet thought that in love always sees
as if to measure distances. It is nakedness where all
that cannot die gathers. It is all beauty held.
It is the hand or the soul wounded with love by another hand.
An aching bramble bush that dreams of counting caresses.
It sleeps little and watches over what is small, light and frail.
It takes peace lightly, as if unworthy.
It stops happiness, knowing what that means.
Maybe nothing is simple if lost illusions
do not wound it. Maybe nothing changes without longing or the wind.
Simplicity, if I were to love again now, I would love you again.
But give me your spirit and grow firm in my firm strength.
Simplicity is saying your beloved name that is like the rain.

Si pudiera

Ayer posé mi mano y mi aire en el aire de la fuente
y un inmenso recuerdo fue la tarde. Me encontré mi risa
y era una tarde de mayo. Toqué el dolor de lo lejano,
de lo que fue y no fue, y de lo que fue y no supe saber que era;
el dolor de estar lejos del romero, o de mí, o de ti, o de algo,
y los dedos fueron sumida ensoñación, inmenso olor
el agua. A veces pienso que toda mi vida es un olor:
a silencio, a madre en el tallo de la rosa, a amor antiguo,
a trigo que despierta con la luna, a presa de los sueños.
Yo no sé. Toqué el dolor del sueño que nunca es lo soñado,
y la noche fue cigüeña de bronce sin luz en mis hombros,
vuelo dormido en mi vuelo, vuelo de sangre en mi savia.
Si supiera. Si pudiera, al menos, posar lenta en el verso,
posar la vida en el verso lento, posar el verso en el verso.
Si pudiera posar desnuda de mí para el mar, para el río,
para el cielo. Si pudiera posar, sólo posar en silencio.

If I Could Only

Yesterday I rested my hand and my air on the fountain's air
and the afternoon was an immense memory. I found my laughter
and it was a May afternoon. I touched the pain of distance,
of what was and was not, of what was but I knew it not;
the pain of being far away from rosemary, from me or you, or something.
My fingers were dreaming underground, water
an immense smell. Sometimes I think my whole life is this smell:
of silence, of mother in the rose stem, of an old love,
of wheat that wakes with the moon, the prey of dreams.
I do not know. I touched the pain of a dream that is never dreamed,
and night was a bronze stork dark on my shoulders,
flight asleep in my flight, a flight of blood in the sap.
If I only knew. If I could only, at least, rest slowly in poetry,
rest life in slow poetry, rest poetry in poetry.
If I could only rest free of myself for the sea, for the river,
for the sky. If I could rest, only rest in silence.

Pensar la tarde

Una plaza de tilos, una nube clara, un pájaro
sin nido, un nido que arropa al agua que se convierte
en cielo, un oler lento, un decir fuego y ser magnolia,
un estar, una razón de ser que espera a la noche,
una luz que tiembla cadenciosa como la miel
de uvas tiernas, un acaso, un tal vez: esto es la tarde.
Esto es la tarde: un minuto de fragancia precisa,
un saber que voy a quererte, cada día más,
con más nostalgia sin respuestas; un querer quererte
en movimiento y un soñar amarte detenida.

Thinking Late Afternoon

A plaza of lime trees, clear cloud, bird
without a nest wrapping water that changes
into sky, a slow scent, a saying fire and being magnolia,
a being there. A reason for being waits for night,
a light trembles in cadence like the honey
of tender grapes, a perchance or perhaps: this is late afternoon.
This is late afternoon: a minute of precise fragrance,
a knowing I will love you, every day more,
with more longing, with no answers. A wanting to love you
moves and a dream of loving you is ended.

Silencio

Concha de mar, madre del silencio, caricia del sonido,
en ti se abre, se desdobla, crece la eternidad del gesto,
de tu gesto que puja alto por mis sueños, por mi silencio.
Silencio, padre del alma, hospedería del paso, espejo
del labio, a ti vuelvo, lagar de sombras, examen de encuentros.
A ti vuelvo por mi ausencia, con mi gesto de rojo olivo
que te ciñe y ciñe tu libranza, y esta luna es invierno
y estas manos, silencio, son mis manos y mi amor, tu acecho.
¿En qué palabra, en qué rumor, en qué arroyo escondo mi vida,
en qué tiempo escondo flores y cieno, en qué arrayán el verso?
En todo me oculto, amor, y en nada te me ocultas, y en todo
me detienes y en nada te detengo: sólo en el silencio.

Silence

Shell from the sea, mother of silence, sound caressed,
in you the eternity of gesture opens, unfolds,
your gesture pushes deep into my dreams, my silence.
Silence, father of the soul, asylum of footsteps, mirrored
lips, to you I return, winepress of shadows, examination of encounters.
I return to you for my absence, with my gesture like the red olive tree
that goes round and round your liberty. This moon is winter
and these hands, silence, are my hands and my love, your stalking.
In what word, in what rumor, in what stream do I hide my life,
in what time do I hide flowers and sky, in what myrtle poetry?
I hide myself, love, in every thing. You hide from me in nothing.
You hold me in everything, and I hold you in nothing: only in silence.

Historia de abril. Entonces

Como si nada hubiera sucedido, como si nada hubiera
pasado, me llamaste como quien cambia el curso de los árboles,
como quien trueca aliento por sueños, pan tierno por esperanzas.
Escribes lejanías con flores, flor del algodón, me dices,
viviendo, muriendo así de nostalgias, muriendo de nostalgia.
Viniste a mí como un río buscando el arroyo. Y no hay arroyo.
Buscando el arroyo de mis manos. Manos que sombras, que brasas
sustentan. Sólo sombras de adioses, sólo brasas de
    frío asedio.
Nuestro viaje más largo: encuentro de desencuentros consumados,
ejercicio de ballestas, pelo cano, sinrazón de tiempo,
el tiempo que llevas prendido en los labios, atado en el alma,
tiempo que no te conoce, tiempo que tú olvidaste en la fuente.
Qué callado dolor el tuyo, qué ajeno a ti siendo tuyo,
qué ajeno a mí siendo en lo mío, rosetón dormido, acacia.
Como si nada fuera a suceder, como si nada, viniste
a mi cuerpo rompiendo saetas, quebrando tu alma en mis trenzas,
quebrando amores en mi alma, naves que fueron sueños, que fueron.
Te fuiste como un volcán, como un barco que lleva el universo,
como una ausencia imaginaria, naufragio de alegrías, manos,
misterio cumplido, melancolía. ¡Y tú me hablas de nostalgia!
Te fuiste. Como nada, como si nada hubiera sucedido.

April History. Then

As if nothing had happened, as if nothing
had passed, you called me as if to change the flow of trees,
or switch breath for dreams, tender bread for hopes.
You write remote places with flowers, cotton flowers, you tell me,
living, hence dying of longings, dying of longing.
You came to me like a river seeking the stream. And there is no stream.
Seeking the stream of my hands. Hands that feed
shadows, burning coals. Only shadows of farewells, only the coals of a
    cold siege.
Our longest trip: an encounter of consummated non-encounters,
an exercise of crossbows, gray hair, crazed time,
time you caught on your lips, tied to your soul,
time that does not know you, time that you forgot at the fountain.
How quiet your pain, so alien to you though yours,
so alien to me though mine, though the sleep of stained glass, or acacia.
As if nothing would happen, nothing, you came
to my body breaking arrows, splitting your soul in my hair,
splitting love in my soul, ships that were dreams, that were.
You left like a volcano, like a boat taking the universe,
like an imaginary absence, shipwreck of joy, hands,
mystery ended, melancholy. And you talk to me about longing!
You left. Like nothing, like nothing had happened.

From: *Intacto asombro en la luz del silencio*
(*Astonishment Intact in the Light of Silence*)

Dominio del recuerdo

Recordar es siempre un invierno largo abriendo lento el trigo,
abriendo sagaz la vida en verso, cerrando el todo en nada,
abriendo en marfil el árbol, cerrando el azahar en muslos,
abriendo, cerrando el arado, la voz curvada en la tierra.
Dios del pan y el verso, es claro invierno y alguien corta
    las ramas
y alguien pierde los sueños y alguien—¿quién?—se levanta del sueño
—del sueño de ser naranjo hecho hombre y dulce verbo en llamas—,
y alguien se talla en rosas y alguien deshoja la bronca carne
de los cipreses y bebe el agua que bebieron las fuentes.
Recuerdo, tragaluz del vino, batea de llanto, alfarje
de sangre, blanca concha, ciego y rudo remero de flores;
cruza los nardos, recuerdo, cruza los nardos sin angustia:
su blanca flor lleva el instante y naves llenas de corceles;
deja tu espada, recuerdo, la espada en el centro del sueño,
en la cima del heno, en la brasa del llanto sobre el agua:
su estatismo rompe el tiempo en prados, las lunas en rediles;
corta la uva más dulce del camino, sueño, la más leve,
que el sueño exige cantarada para hablar con cada sueño,
que la vida nos pide agua para beber la vida en sueños.
Recordar cuando es recuerdo es dominio del aire y el sosiego,
recordar cuando es sueño es la vida entrando lenta en rojo trigo.

Dominion of Memory

Remembering is always a long winter slowly opening the wheat,
opening life wisely into poetry, enclosing everything into nothing,
opening the tree into ivory, enclosing orange blossoms into thighs,
opening, enclosing the plough, the voice curved in the earth.
God of bread and poetry, plain winter is here and someone is cutting
    the branches
and someone is losing dreams and someone—who?—rises from a dream
—the dream of an orange tree become a man and a sweet word in flames—
and someone is cutting into roses and someone is peeling the wild flesh
of cypress and drinking the water that fountains swallowed.
Memory, a skylight of wine, trough of tears, millstone
of blood, white shell, the rough, blind oarsman rowing flowers.
Memory crosses the spikenards, calmly crosses the spikenards:
its white flower bears the moment and ships full of horses.
Leave your sword, memory, the sword in the heart of the dream,
on the crown of the hay, in the burning coal of weeping over water:
its immobility breaks time into meadows, moons into sheepfolds.
Dream cutting the sweetest grape on the road, and the lightest,
for the dream requires flowing pitchers in order to speak with each dream,
for life asks water of us in order to drink life in dreams.
To remember memory is dominion over air and stillness.
To remember a dream is life entering slowly into the red wheat.

Amor, hondura de la sed

Amor, hondura de piedra más allá de la hondura del tiempo,
hondura de lumbre, hondura del ala más allá del espacio,
hondura simple multiplicada por el rocío en el árbol
del sueño, por el azahar prendido entre frutos y alegría,
por la palabra que sube al manantial y vuela y se detiene
en un cuenco de escarcha e inocencia, en un cuenco de pan y leche,
en una frente que corre por los lirios buscando su hondura.
Amor de amor, dulce mirador del hombre, súbeme a tus ojos,
súbeme otra vez a tus sueños porque en el amor nada basta,
ni siquiera el aire de la silva es suficiente para el fuego,
ni las manos son manos del ser si no las enciendes con tu aire;
súbeme al pecho de la lluvia, a la armonía, a tu paz abierta
en cerezas de luna, a tu voz bien temperada en plenitudes;
súbeme a un pensar sereno y bájame la frente a los sentidos.
Amor, hondura de mi hondura, este del cuerpo, norte del alba,
sal en la cancela de mi sangre, miel en la reja de asombros,
dentro de ti me busco: en la dulce simetría de tus ramas,
en la fuerza de la belleza, en tu tiempo que no cumple al tiempo;
dentro de mí te busco y tu silencio responde a mi silencio.

Love, Deep Thirst

Love, deep stone beyond deep time,
deep light, deep wing beyond space,
simple depth multiplied by the dew on the tree
of sleep, by orange blossoms caught between fruit and joy,
by the word that rises to the source and soars and stops
in a bowl of frost and innocence, in a bowl of bread and milk,
in a face that runs through irises seeking the depths.
Love of loves, sweet balcony of man, lift me to your eyes.
Lift me to your dreams because with love nothing is enough.
Not even sylvan air is enough for fire,
nor are hands the hands of being unless you burn them with your air.
Lift me to the rain's breast, to harmony, to your peace opening
in the cherry moon, to your voice well-tempered in plenitude.
Lift me to serene thought and lower my face to the senses.
Love, depth of my depths, east of the body, north of the dawn,
salt in the lattice gate of my blood, honey in the iron grates of astonishment,
in you I seek myself: in the sweet symmetry of your branches,
in the strength of beauty, in your time that does not complete time;
in myself I seek you. Your silence responds to my silence.

Un cuerpo, el sur

Cuánto vino amaestrado en la lengua resuena en los ríos,
cuánto vino descendiendo por la sed, por la cal de los muros,
por el sur que siempre interroga al labio o descansa en el beso,
el sur—luna llena en la boca, circe de luz, circe del tiempo—
que hunde siempre la boca, la luz, el tiempo o el beso en la tierra
y la tierra asciende por el hombre y el hombre vuelve a los sueños.
Cuánta alma en el labio, cuánta hoja en sombra escondida ante los ojos,
cuánto dolor acuñado en oro, cuánto pensamiento en bronce,
cuánto de todo en barro que hasta la misma sed es pura arcilla.
Es tarde de mayo y una sed de sol en la piedra me encierra
—como la sed de un niño que es más sed porque la llora
    o la canta—,
me daña como pintura de la tarde en lugar de la tarde,
como partitura del aire en lugar del aire mismo en su aire.
Tarde y alguien se talla en rosas y alguien se levanta del sueño
—del sueño de ser naranjo hecho hombre y dulce verbo en llamas—
para hundir su dura sed en la tierra y volver a sus sueños.
Cuánto sueño amaestrado en la lengua, amor, cuánto sueño y vino:
me tiendo en tu cuerpo—un cuerpo siempre es sur—y descanso en el beso.

A Body, the South

So much well-taught wine on the tongue resounds in rivers,
so much wine descending from thirst, from walls of lime,
from the south forever questioning lips or resting in a kiss,
the south—full moon in a mouth, Circe of light, Circe of time—
forever plunging the mouth, light, time, the kiss in the earth,
and the earth rises for man and man returns to dreams.
So much soul on lips, so many leaves in the shadow hidden from the eyes,
so much pain minted into gold, so much thought into bronze,
so much of everything muddied. Even thirst itself is pure clay.
A May afternoon, and thirst like the sun in stone encases me
—like the thirst of a child being more thirst because he cries and sings
    for it—
wounds me like a painting of the afternoon instead of the afternoon,
like a musical score of the air instead of the air itself in air.
Afternoon, and someone is cutting into roses and someone rises from a dream
—the dream of an orange tree become a man and a sweet word in flames—
to sink hard thirst in the earth and return to dreams.
So many well-taught dreams on the tongue, love, so many dreams and wine:
I stretch out in your body—a body is always south—and sleep in the kiss.

Recogido asombro

Casi sentir y pensar son lo mismo, no a la luz del recuerdo
como esperé, sino a la luz de mayo en celosías de ensueño;
casi silencio y agua son lo mismo, casi tierra y silencio
tienen parecida forma, los mismos verdes, las mismas flores;
casi la vida, fuerza de soledad, recoge amor y fuerza
en un mismo río de frutos y espera donde el alma duerme.
Me recojo en asombros, me desnudo de puentes y rosales,
me siento entre el yo y el nido—pensarse entre el sentir
   y el pensar—
y encuentro la palabra arrancando acantos de luna a las noches
de azahar, el deseo sonoro en flor al dolor del deseo,
—y el amor se esconde porque es amor buscarlo siempre y no hallarlo
y hallarlo dormido entre piedra y luna a la altura de los sueños—;
y encuentro entre carne y hueso la tarde, entre zaguanes y acacias
el llanto, y la ternura—ah, esta ternura—entre el aire y el tiempo.
Me busco entre el verso—asilo del romero, agua alta y detenida—,
me busco, y ya no me oculto ni oculto los ríos de mi brazo
ni mi mano perdida en el cuerpo, ni mi pie entre tierra y lanza,
ni el arroyo—silencio de la vida—entre un nombre y su silencio.
Me sueño porque es hermoso soñarse para cuando no importen
los sueños, o importen tanto que sean saber de alma dormida,
de alma despierta, conciliación, de alma hacia un sentir sobre
   el alma.
Casi sentir—circe de jazmín con vino—y pensar—azafrán
de fuego—y soñar—rosario vivo de azabache—son lo mismo;
casi tarde y rosetón son la misma luz, casi mano y alma
son la misma risa en los jardines, la misma flor en los patios;
casi somos lo mismo encina, cántaro y barro detenido.
Como mayo—celosía del tiempo, dulce y blanco trigal
en lo desnudo—, el ser se acerca a la palabra y tiende a sus sueños.

Quiet Astonishment

To feel and to think are nearly the same, not in the light of memory
as I expected, but in the light of May in the lattice work of dreams.
Silence and water are nearly the same, earth and silence
have nearly a similar shape, the same green, the same flowers.
Life nearly, the strength of solitude, holds love and strength
in the same river of fruit and waits where the soul sleeps.
I gather my astonished self, I disrobe bridges and rosebushes,
I sit between myself and a nest—thinking oneself between feeling
    and thought—
and I find the word tearing out acanthus of the moon from orange blossom
nights, the echo of flowering desire from the pain of desire
—and love hides because love is always sought and not found
or found asleep between stone and moon in the zone of dreams.
I discover the afternoon between flesh and bone, weeping between corridors
and acacias, and tenderness—ah, this tenderness—between air and time.
I look for myself in poetry—an asylum of rosemary, high waters held back—
I look for myself, no more hiding the rivers of my arm
or my hand lost in the body, or my foot between earth and spear,
or the stream—silence of life—between a name and its silence.
I dream myself, it is lovely to dream the self for when dreams
do not matter, or they matter being the wisdom of the soul asleep,
of the soul awake, the two together, of the soul moving toward a sense of
    the soul.
To feel—jasmine Circe with wine—and to think—flaming
saffron—and to dream—living rosary of jet—are nearly the same.
Afternoon and stained glass are nearly the same light, hand and soul
nearly the same laughter in gardens, the same flower in courtyards.
We are nearly the same oak tree, pitcher and molded clay.
Like May—lattice work of time, sweet white fields of wheat
stripped bare—life approaches the word and stretches toward its dreams.

Como mayo, el ser se acerca

Como mayo, el ser se acerca a la palabra y la palabra busca
incesante al ser, un arroyo de aves, una llama de amor,
un olor a río, un cuerpo donde tender sus sueños de tiempo.
Ser y palabra son ya lo mismo: un largo silencio en la hierba.
Déjame, silencio, ser como la palabra—danza de fuego—
y que la palabra sea como yo—danza de agua en la hierba—.

Like May, Life Approaches

Like May, life approaches the word and, incessant,
the word seeks life, birds streaming, love flaming,
the scent of the river, a body tendering dreams of time.
Life and word are the same then: a long silence in the grass.
Let me, silence, be like the word—a dance of fire—
and let the word be like me—a dance of water in the grass.

Canción de aroma

Verano. De pronto, soy mayo todavía con abril
entre las manos. Soy más mayo que mayo y más tiempo que el tiempo.
Soy el lento viento que mece los árboles, y los árboles
son un yo fijo y tierno y un ahora apretado entre los vientos,
y soy frágil sentir y gozar y doler en sentimiento
y un triste pensar acostumbrado que tiembla en luz de piedra.
De pronto, ya no soy ese amor que se mira en las tinajas
de los curtidores, sino el amor que se mira a sí mismo
y se nombra y se mide en acacias, me nombra y me descansa.
Verano y soy un andar despacio por mayo, niño puro,
un andar sereno por aromas y un amor entre los labios.

Scent Song

Summer. Suddenly I am May, with April
still in my hands. I am more May than May and more time than time itself.
I am the slow wind that rocks the trees, and the trees
are me, steady and tender, a dense air-born now,
and I am a fragile sensing, pleasure and pain inside feeling
and sad, habitual thought trembling in the stone-light.
Suddenly, I am no longer that love looking inside the tanners'
earthen jars, but love looking at itself,
that names and measures itself in acacias, that names and gives me sleep.
Summer, and I am a slow walking in May, pure child,
a serene walking in scents and love on my lips.

A veces, el presente es

A veces, me sorprendo soñándome con tu esplendor en mis sueños
—en cada flor la mano, en cada piedra el alma, en cada jarro
sin asa la perfumada soledad, en cada dura orilla
la templanza, en cada abrazo la verdad, en cada fruto el cielo,
en cada copla el infierno de lo que nunca pudo decirse—,
me sorprendo soñándome con un soñar lento hacia arriba,
—cuando andes deprisa, teme al agua en la sequía: la víbora
acecha como el rayo en el olivo, el tiempo en lo que hace el tiempo—,
y no quiero soñarme ni soñarte, sino vivir y andarte
como se vive lo lejano sin saber que es lejanía:
nunca volveré a buscarme allí donde dejé una altura de sueños.
Presente, sabiduría interior, camino hacia la mansedumbre,
quiero ser como el trigo al viento: remolino de cielo, tierra
firme, nube de lluvia, pan para el hambre de amor, altura
cifrada, infinitud recogida en tiempo, y finitud sin carencia
—el niño muerde la luna creyendo que es un vuelo de cisne,
así muerdo el verso para olvidar la manzana que hirió la lumbre—.
Presente, te aparto el tiempo que te sobra y te doy el que te falta:
abro caminos para el tiempo por donde fluya sin rozar
al alma, donde se estreche como un junco buscando la luz,
donde se ensanche como un monte, un campo, un azul en la pintura.
Presente, te busco y creo al amor en la piedra para tu búsqueda
—sabrás su amor por su manera de recoger el espliego,
conocerás su alma por su manera de cortar el agua—,
te busco en mis límites, me pierdo entre conocimiento
    y tristeza;
me busco y encuentro la nada donde algo debió ocurrir
y no ocurrió, donde algo no debió ocurrir y ocurrió
    sin dicha;
me busco en ti y encuentro la paz, mansedumbre, sueño de tu sueño;
busco a quien mide, a quien canta lo hondo y te encuentro en un
    vuelo de cisne.
A veces, me sorprendo: la hierba se detiene en la boca
del aire, y lo que fue y lo que será son sólo eterno presente.

Sometimes, Now Is

Sometimes, I surprise myself dreaming of your splendor in my dreams
—in every flower the hand, in every stone the soul, in every pitcher
without a handle perfumed solitude, in every hard shore
a tempering, in every embrace the truth, in every fruit the sky,
in every song the hell of what could never be said.
I surprise myself dreaming a slow dream upward:
walk quickly, fear water in a drought. The viper
strikes like lightning on the olive tree, time on what makes time.
I do not want to dream myself or you, but to live and walk as you
the way you live distance not knowing it is distance:
I will never look for myself again where I left a summit of dreams.
Now is, inner wisdom, gentle road,
I want to be like wheat to the wind: swirls of sky, terra
firma, rain cloud, bread for the hunger of love, perfected
height, infinity gathered in time, bags and bags of the finite.
The child bites the moon and believes it is a swan flying,
as I bite poetry to forget the apple in the wound of light.
Now is, I separate left-over time from you and give you what is missing:
I open roads for time to flow like light against
the soul, where it narrows like a reed seeking light,
where it spreads like a mountain, a field, the blue of a painting.
Now is, I look for you creating love in the stone for you to seek.
You will know love by its way of gathering lavender,
you will know the soul by its way of cutting through water.
I look for you in my limits, losing myself somewhere between knowing
    and sadness;
I look for myself, finding the void where something ought to have happened
and did not happen, where something unlucky ought not to have happened
    and happened.
I look for myself in you and I find peace, gentleness, the dream of your dream.
I look for someone to measure, someone to sing deep and I find you in a
    swan flying.
Sometimes, I surprise myself: grass is held in the mouth
of air, and what was and what will be are only an eternal now.

El tiempo distinto de cada ausencia

Luz de otoño, rosa, azul y aire, tanta belleza sin culpa
culpando al hombre de ojos de cuervo, escarcha, espalda de barro
en el amor, alma de lanza, lengua de viento y baraja,
lágrima de láudano apoyada en el cierzo, diente de opio,
azafrán y vino para mentir su vida y en racimos
elevar la ausencia, el rocío, contra los verdes y mares.
El hombre ciego de tiempo, ciego el pecho de arroyos claros,
es culpable de vivir su tiempo—navaja descansada—
y no el tiempo de la luz en los ojos, el correr del agua,
los lugares, cada lugar que juega con aire a los sueños.
Luz de otoño, el hombre no cabe en ti con sus manos de grana,
con sus muros, con su amor, sus pies encendidos—cada calle
tiene su besar—, con la permanencia robada en los dientes.
No cabe en sí mismo. No cabe en la vida. No cabe tanto
azul y rosa en su pecho de arroyo, tanto aire en su tiempo.
¿Cómo aprender a vivir el tiempo de las cosas, las calles,
los muelles, los besos con nuestro tiempo apoyado en el tiempo?
¿Cómo aprender a ser el tiempo distinto de cada tierra,
de cada cosa y cada cuerpo? Respiración en la cerca.
Tiempo sereno que, a veces, me serenas, la plenitud
es mi tiempo entrando en el tiempo distinto de cada tiempo.

A Different Time in Every Absence

Autumn light, rose pink, blue and air, so much blameless beauty
to blame the man with crow's eyes, frost, spine of clay
within love, a soul like a spear, a tongue like the wind and confusion,
a laudanum tear held on the north wind, an opium tooth,
saffron and wine to feign his life and elevate absence
in clusters, the dew, against green and the sea.
The man blind with time, his breast blind in clear streams,
is guilty of living his time—tranquil knife—
and not the time of light in the eyes, the running water,
the places, every place that plays dreams with air.
Autumn light, the man won't fit in you with his scarlet hands,
with his walls, with his love, his feet on fire—every street
bears his kisses—stolen permanence in his teeth.
He won't fit in himself. He doesn't fit in life. So much blue
and rose pink cannot fit in his streaming breast, so much air in his time.
How do I learn to live the time of things, streets,
wharfs, kisses with our time held in time?
How do I learn to be different time in every land,
in every thing and every body? The fence breathing.
Serene time, you calm me at times, plenitude
is my time entering time differently every time.

Cerrar para abrir

Cierro el pan para abrir la rosa, el tallo para abrir la paz
—la paz, granada de luna y rumor que abro y golpeo en mi sangre,
que abro en verbos que son manos, que golpeo en piedras que son sueños—,
cierro el hambre de los búhos para abrir mi hambre que restaura
la luz, cierro el color para abrir el sosiego demorado
en la noche, porque, en lo oscuro, azafrán y lengua me asombran.
Me cierro en pan para desnudarme, en hierba para ser carne
que abre el bosque, en fuente para ser piel que roza la inocencia.
Me abro en tiempo para ser un tiempo—cuenco de blanca leche,
de lumbre que alimenta flores, frente, ruiseñor, belleza—,
que me alimenta de hojas, recuerdos y un estar entre arroyos.
Me abro en fuego—no en llamas, la llama viene siempre de fuera—,
me abro los sentidos para alcanzarme donde estoy ahora,
me abro en cedros para ser mi alma, en cerezos para ser cuerpo
de mi cuerpo y cuerpo en ramas donde el silencio brota en tigres.
Cierro las manos—manos de pan y agua—para abrir el verso.

To Enclose is to Open

I enclose the bread to open the rose, the stem to open peace
—peace, pomegranate of moon and rumor opened and beaten in my blood,
that I open in words that are hands, I beat on stones that are dreams—
I enclose the hunger of owls to open my hunger that restores
the light, I enclose color to open tranquility delayed
at night, because, in the dark, saffron and tongue astonish me.
I enclose myself in bread to take off my clothes, in grass to be flesh
that opens the woods, in a fountain to be skin brushing innocence.
I open myself in time to be this time—a bowl of white milk,
of light that feeds flowers, a face, the nightingale, beauty—
that feeds me leaves, memories, flowing in streams.
I open myself in fire—not in flames, the flame always comes from without—
I open my senses to find where I am now.
I open myself in cedar to be my soul, in cherry trees to be the body
of my body, the body in branches where silence breaks into tigers.
I close my hands—hands of bread and water—to open the poem.

Pared blanca, fluyo en voz por vuestro silencio

Pared blanca, interior del cansancio, alforja y muslo de la vida,
litoral del cuerpo oscurecido en madrigueras y palabras,
laberinto donde la infancia tiene forma de dalia y voz
de limón desnudado, limón que enseña al cuervo la ternura.
Pido tregua confiada—ternura y tiempo, alacena
    mentida—
para reposar cuanto aprendí y rocé en las noches de mi cuerpo.
Pared blanca halladora de palomas donde no se refleja
la certidumbre ni el recuerdo, adiéstrame en olvido y blancura,
adiestra mi cesta con pan sobre la mesa, mi angustia, el gesto
que cifra azul con esa jarra de leche derramando el tiempo
—porque eso es el tiempo puro, establo de eternidad redimida,
porque eso es intimidad, el brazo más desnudo con la luz—,
derramando el fuego, los versos, las rosas bajo los pies de agua.
Adiestra el cuenco que sostengo, el amor que me sostiene en vasos,
mi amor, mi prisa, mi tardanza, el clavo donde un día hubo tiempo.
Adiestra mi sonrisa—¿durará tu sonrisa en algún cuerpo,
en alguna parte a la que yo no puedo llegar con mi olvido?—,
adiestra mi sonrisa—peso del mundo, levedad del alma—,
que no quiero vivir en vano y el peso es demasiado grande
para mi labio, y la levedad muy pequeña para mis sombras.
Adiéstrame en queda donación—dime que nada ha sido inútil—,
adiéstrame en la luz y aceptaré el badil de hojas que me espera,
el recuerdo que me tuerce, el dolor que me adiestra en mis sembrados.
De hecho, no ocurre nada. Sólo mi vieja y frondosa costumbre
de temer al aire y temer al trino del júbilo asombrado.
Es mi frente de patios, es la abeja de mis manos, el pulso
de mi miedo, el mirto de mis ojos los que tiemblan sobre el pan,
los que sueñan una tregua ajena al sueño henchido de mi cuerpo.
Pared blanca, espejo de cal serena, lecho de agua y silencio,
brazos que soportáis mis ramas, que imitáis los ríos serenos,
fluyo en voz por vuestro silencio, en sombra y luz, luz en
    vuestra luz.

White Wall, I Flow in the Voice Because of Your Silence

White wall, the inside of exhaustion, saddlebag and sinew of life,
coast of the body darkened in burrows and words,
labyrinth where childhood is a dahlia and the voice
of a peeled lemon, the lemon that teaches tenderness to the crow.
I ask for the confidence of truce—tenderness and time, a make-believe
    cupboard—
to digest what I learned and barely touched in the nights of my body.
White wall, detector of doves where neither certainty nor memory's
reflected, teach me forgetting and whiteness,
teach my bread basket on the table, my anguish, the sign
that adds blue with that pitcher of milk spilling time
—because that is pure time, a stable of redeemed eternity,
that is intimacy, the arm barest with light—
spilling fire, verses, roses beneath the water's feet.
Teach the bowl I hold, the love that sustains me with a glass,
my love, my haste, my lateness, the nail where once there was time.
Teach my smile—will your smile last in some body,
somewhere I cannot reach with my amnesia?
Teach my smile—weight of the world, lightness of the soul—
I do not want to live in vain and the weight is too great
for my lips, and the lightness very small for my shadows.
Teach me the quiet gift—tell me that nothing has been futile—
teach me the light and I will accept the fire shovel of leaves that waits,
the memory that twists me, the pain that teaches me in the furrows of fields.
In truth, nothing is happening. Only my old luxuriant habit
of fearing the air, the chant of astonished joy.
My face is like a courtyard, my hands the bee, the pulse
of my fear, the myrtle of eyes trembling over bread,
dreaming a truce apart from the swollen dream of my body.
White wall, serene mirror of lime, bed of water and silence,
arms that support my branches, imitate serene rivers,
I flow in the voice because of your silence, in the shadow and light, light in
    your light.

La luz entra por el verso

La luz entra por mi cuerpo y la angustia, el amor y la nieve,
y me alejo de mí y me acerco y son siempre la misma angustia,
el mismo amor, la misma luz y nieve . . . y un cuerpo distinto.
¿Cómo retenerlo todo si el cuerpo permanece y llora,
si el cisne florido no puede rozar la hoja del ciruelo?
¿Cómo retenerlo todo si el cuerpo de amor sólo vive
su altura en la altura de otro cuerpo y su vida en su otra vida?
¿Cómo vivirte más, sentirte más, amor, si sólo tengo
dos ojos negros en la nieve y unas manos en tus sueños?
¿Cómo ser más, tarde, agua, alondra, cielo, si mi única sangre
sólo está sembrada de mirlos y de miedo, y sólo tengo
un arroyo de fe en alguna parte y una frágil puerta
a la nostalgia que desciende por la espalda, por la espada
que dobla la eternidad en mares, rebaños y naranjos
—¿por qué?, busca en ti lo que queda de ti en cada tarde tuya—,
si sólo guardo una fuente en alguna parte y sólo quiero
el recuerdo de un jardín con nieve cubierto por tus manos,
por tus manos de dulce bosque y claro nombre en dulce pecho,
que pueden cubrir el sol, mi cuerpo, la soledad sin sol?
¿Cómo ser más en mí contigo si amor y belleza se unen,
cómo ser alma y cuerpo sin que se confundan,
sin que me confundan en volar y yacer al mismo tiempo?
¿Cómo ser más, amor, si sólo tengo un sueño repartido
por el cuerpo y mi cuerpo se reparte grano por tus sueños?
¿Cómo ser más sin ser otra cosa si mi vida ya se abre
en palomas por mi frente y mi hogar tiene ya un río, un nombre?
La luz entra por el verso, y cuerpo, alma y tarde son distintos.

Light Enters through Poetry

Light enters my body, anguish, love and snow.
I move away from myself, come closer and it is always the same anguish,
the same love, the same light and snow . . . and a different body.
How do I hold everything if the body remains and cries,
if the flowering swan cannot brush the leaf of the plum tree?
How do I hold everything if the body of love only lives
its intensity in the intensity of another body and its life in another life?
How do I live you more, feel you more, love, if all I have
are two dark eyes in the snow and hands in your dreams?
How to be more, to be afternoon, water, lark, sky, if my blood only
is seeded with black birds and fear, and somewhere
all I have is a stream of faith and a fragile door
to the longing that slides down the back, down the sword
that folds eternity into seas, flocks and orange trees
—Why? Look inside yourself for what remains of all your days—
if all I hold is a fountain somewhere and all I want
is the memory of a garden with snow covered by your hands,
by your sweet wooded hands and a clear name in a sweet breast,
to cover the sun, my body, sunless solitude?
How to be more in myself with you when love and beauty unite,
how to be body and soul and not confuse them,
not confuse flying and being still at the same time?
How to be more, love, if all I have is a dream shared
by the body and my body shares out grain in your dreams?
How to be more and not be something else if my life already is opening
into doves as though my face, and my home already has a river, a name?
Light enters through poetry, and body, soul, and afternoon have changed.

Cierre del ciclo de la nieve

Nada se distancia en mí tanto como la paz, nada se acerca
a mí tanto como los sueños, nada tanto como la nieve.
Fui un jardín con nieve, un rosal con nieve, una escalera con nieve,
escaleras de piedra y musgo y nieve que daban a mi mano,
escaleras que subían de la piedra al musgo, de mi frente
a la vida de mis sueños, que bajaban de mi sueño al mundo.
Fue felicidad. Fui estoque de niñez en la tierra, fui cinco
dedos en las flores y un cuerpo pequeño en mi ave ante la vida,
fui algo que ya no soy y soy algo que ya no seré nunca.
Y duele, dueles como fresno en las mejillas, como mordiente
en los bosques, como lugar hermoso que es viaje hacia la nieve.
Cuerpo mío que me abandonas a cada instante y permaneces,
¿cómo retenerte en las flores, cómo tenerte sin tus sombras?
No me bastas cuerpo mío—piel y voz con nieve—,
   no me basta
con tu cuerpo que habita la soledad del tiempo y de las aguas:
sólo aguas y amor te darán un soplo de universo en las piedras.
Nada se distancia en mí tanto como mi cuerpo, como beso
que resbala por la nieve, y es amor el valle, y cumbre el cuerpo.
Nada se acerca a mí tanto como un nombre, su paz en mi boca.

Closing the Cycle of Snow

Nothing is more remote in me than peace, nothing is closer
to me than dreams, nothing more than snow.
I was a garden with snow, a rose bush with snow, stairs with snow,
stairs of stone and moss and snow extending to my hand,
stairs that climbed from stone to moss, from my face
to the life of my dreams, and descended from my sleep to the world.
It was happiness. I was a sword of childhood thrust in the earth, I was five
fingers in the flowers and a small bird body facing life.
I was something I no longer am and I am something I will no longer ever be.
And it hurts, you hurt like the whip of ash on cheeks, like scissors
in the woods, like a place of beauty traveling toward snow.
Body of mine, you leave me constantly and yet remain.
How to hold on to you and flowers, how to hold you and not your shadows?
You are not enough, body of mine—the snow of skin and voice—you are
    not enough
with your body that lives the solitude of time and water:
only water and love will give you the breath of the universe in stones.
Nothing is more remote in me than my body, than the kiss
slipping through snow, love is the valley, and summit the body.
Nothing is closer to me than a name, its peace in my mouth.

Cerco seco de mi nombre

Esta cárcel tiene un nombre y no sé qué tenso nombre tiene
que cuando me acerco se hace carne y cuando me alejo, espíritu.
Esta cárcel tiene un aquí y un allá donde el ruido escarcha
la belleza, y la angustia corre libre y ancha como un ciervo.
Os hablo de cárcel y angustia, dos palabras sin silencio,
dos caminos que son mi orilla izquierda y mi llanto derecho.
Os hablo de la angustia, palabra que nada significa,
junco que nada necesita, andanza que nada precisa.
El mar es pozo de nenúfares comparado a este junco.
Junco pasivo al vaivén de la belleza, acre atormentado,
añil sufrido, que se revelan como el viento en la cumbre.
Os hablo de la angustia que deja sin testigo a los rostros,
que deja a los sueños como dama de escarcha ante la escarcha,
de la angustia aprisionada en el té como un círculo de agua,
de huesos sin mirra ni morada, como un callar hablado.
Esta cárcel tiene un nombre antiguo, dolor de muchos nombres,
y no sé en qué cerco seco de mi nombre encontrar su nombre.

Dry Circle of my Name

This jail has a name but I do not know what tense it has
that when I am near it is flesh and when I am far, spirit.
This jail has a here and an over there where noise turns beauty
to frost, and anguish runs free and wild like a deer.
I speak to you of jail and anguish, two words without silence,
two roads that are my left shore and my right crying.
I speak to you of anguish, a word that signifies nothing,
a reed that wants nothing, a fate that requires nothing.
The sea is a well of water lilies compared to this reed.
Passive reed waving to and fro in beauty, bitter torment,
the cloth of patience, a revelation like the wind in the mountains.
I speak to you of anguish that leaves faces without witnesses,
that leaves dreams like a woman of frost before the frost,
of anguish imprisoned in tea like a circle of water,
of bones without myrrh or home, like a low murmuring.
This jail has an old name, the pain of many names.
I do not know in what dry circle of my name I might find its name.

Tuviste mapas de otros ríos

Tuviste mapas de otros ríos más tranquilos, más serenos,
que no seguiste, que no cruzaste el claro hilo de sus aguas,
porque su caudal era hermoso y tuviste miedo de herirte,
de herirlo, de herir a los que mienten rotundos desde el alba.
Tuviste un mapa de bellezas y otro de suaves tristezas,
un mapa de amor que te pareció escollo, alto pergamino
de los dioses, y fue un adiós tu aliento y un adiós tu mano
mecida en el recuerdo, un mapa de recuerdos que olvidaste.
Quién pudiera olvidar tanto si fuera a mantenerse en paz,
pero el precio, el del olvido, son ojos sin luna entre hierba,
ojos tiernos entre patas de lobos, hombre y madreselva.
Grano a grano pudiste ser feliz, pero no lo sabías,
pero no encontraste tu voz en el fruto, tu eco en la carne
del fruto que escuchaba tu voz, pero nunca respondía.
¿Quién eras tú para el fruto?, ¿quién eras tú para la luz?
¿Quién te negó el día y la noche, quién con ellos trazó un hilo
oscuro de dientes que no eran río, sino agua de muerte?
Acercaste el marfil entre tus brazos, el marfil del tiempo
usado por los otros, la soledad que el otro dejaba
perdida en la ribera, y tú la recogías como a un hijo.
Cuántos hijos, ¿verdad?, cuántas soledades y diente en brasa
recoge el hombre en el hombre, cuánto puño y hoja cerrada.
Tu casa, un chopo sin luna como tus ojos, dulce chopo
de caballos recogidos en el mar—el mar, tu templanza—,
el mar demasiado pequeño para tus sueños de entonces,
porque entonces era entonces y era tiempo y dolor florido.
No pienses. Tu chopo, tu casa de caballos permanecen,
y permanece tu mano, la del adiós, que sólo cubre
tus ojos, que sólo te cubre los ojos cuando el silencio
es tormenta de hojas y la hoja un vino amargo del incienso,
—no matarás la dulce cancela que elegí entre los hombres—.
Paciente, como las siembras, te recoges, cierras los pies,
abres los pies de los otros, que fueron azada en tu lecho.
Así es el dolor: un lecho, un cuerpo que nunca te recoge,
un trigo que contempla a las lavanderas sin dios, un trigo,
una ternura en la piedra, un mover las mieses con los sueños.
¿Quién pudo levantar su voz como tierra enjuta en tu hierba?
¿Quién secó las fuentes donde bebías el agua y la luz?
¿Quién levantó en su prisa la misericordia de mirarte?

You Had Maps of Other Rivers

You had maps of other rivers more tranquil and serene,
you did not follow. You did not cross the clear thread of waters,
because the flow was lovely and you were afraid of wounding yourself,
of wounding it, of wounding those flat-out liars at daybreak.
You had a map of beauty and another of soft sadness,
a map of love that seemed to you a reef, the exalted parchment
of the gods, and your breath was a farewell and farewell your hand
rocked in memory, a map of memories that you forgot.
Who could forget so much just to keep peace.
The price of forgetting is moonless eyes in the grass,
tender eyes among the feet of wolves, men and honeysuckle.
Grain by grain you might have been happy, but you knew not,
you could not find your voice in the fruit, your echo in the flesh
of the fruit your voice heard, but never answered.
What were you for the fruit? For the light?
Who severed you from day and night, who traced with them a dark
thread of teeth that was not a river, but the water of death?
You held ivory close in your arms, someone else's
ivory time, the solitude someone else abandoned
and lost on the shore, and you gathered it up as though a child.
So many children, no? So many solitudes and teeth aching
does man collect from man, so many fists and closed blades.
Your house, a black poplar moonless like your eyes, sweet poplar
of horses assembled in the sea—your well-tempered sea—
the sea was too small for your dreams then,
because that was then and it was time and flowering grief.
Do not think. Your poplar, your house of horses remain,
and your hand remains, waving good-bye, covering
your eyes, only covering your eyes when silence
is a leaf storm and the leaf a bitter wine of incense
—you won't kill the sweet lattice gate I chose among men.
Patiently, like sowing, you collect yourself, push your feet together,
spread the feet of others, like a hoe in your bed.
This is pain: a bed, a body that never embraces you,
wheat contemplating laundresses without God, wheat,
a tenderness in the stone, the moving of corn fields with dreams.
Who raised a voice like withered earth in grass?
Who dried the fountains where you drank water and light?
Who rushed to raise compassion looking at you?

¿Quién tiró su última piedra contra tu voz, tu tenue voz
de tan gritada, de tan amansada por tus fieros brazos?
¿Quién levó el cuidado de tu frente?, ¿con qué silencio lo hizo?
Tuviste mapas de otros ríos más tranquilos, más serenos,
¿recuerdas? Hoy, no pienses. Tu chopo, tu casa permanecen.

Who threw the last stone at your voice, faint
from so much shouting, so much soothing in your wild arms?
Who set care on your forehead? With what silence was it done?
You had maps of other rivers more tranquil and serene,
do you remember? For now, do not think. Your poplar, your house remain.

Empiezo donde empieza la palabra

La palabra empieza como ciervo en la boca, como fuente
en la hierba, como fuego en el aire, como aire en los sueños,
como tierra y llama en la boca del ciervo, como una piedra
en las cerezas, como agua en los abetos, como agua y campo
en la voz, en la incertidumbre de la voz en certidumbre,
como un dolor trascendido, ojos, como un sueño no cumplido,
como un tiempo ya cumplido, como un silencio que se cumple.
Palabra y silencio, dolor, lirio, azafrán, casa del aire,
casa del dolor, limosna y riqueza de luz en el pecho,
luz de la misma madre, de la misma espada que divide
la frente en un árbol, el brazo en un río, el alma en las rosas
—¿cómo reuniros si me reúno y el río lleva el árbol
y la rosa el alma y yo me contemplo dividida en miedo?—
y en su centro la vida que corre como corre la angustia,
con ese correr que tiene el todo conmovido en la nada.
Palabra, sálvame de mi espada en el centro de la espada,
de lo oscuro de los nombres que no beben en el silencio.
Silencio, sálvame de la piedra que no sea azahar
en la boca de mi verbo, que no sea luz en la boca
de mis manos, que no sea aire en el hombro puro del fuego.
Palabra, sólo me salvo en ti donde empiezo como un ciervo,
como una fuente, como un sueño en la más clara certidumbre.

I Begin Where the Word Begins

The word begins like a deer in a mouth, like a fountain
in the grass, like fire in air, like air in dreams,
like earth and flame in the mouth of the deer, like a stone
in cherries, like water in firs, like water and field
in the voice, in the uncertainty of the certain voice,
like pain transcended, or eyes, like a dream unconsummated,
like time consummated, like compliant silence.
Word and silence, pain, iris, saffron, house of the air,
house of pain, alms and riches of light in the breast,
light of the mother, of the sword that splits
the face into a tree, the arm into a river, the soul into roses
—how do I gather you up with myself when the river takes the tree
and the rose the soul and I see myself divided in fear?
And in its center life runs like anguish,
with that running that has everything shaken in nothingness.
Word, save me from my sword in the heart of the sword,
from the darkness of names that do not drink in silence.
Silence, save me from the stone that is not orange blossoms
in the mouth of my word, that is not light in the mouth
of my hands, that is not air in the pure shoulder of fire.
Word, I find salvation in you only where I begin like a deer,
like a fountain, like a dream in the clearest certainty.

Loto y rosa en la flor azul

Oratorio de Navidad. Orden del universo y orden
del loto en la luz de la rosa, de la vida sobre el loto.
Junto la boca al recuerdo y desciende lo oscuro y me elevo
como brisa, paz, plenitud, me elevo como lago al este
del manantial, pan, plenitud, la trascendencia ya no hiere.
Oratorio del universo, los pinos son verbo y fuego,
y el aire se remansa en el viento y el agua se detiene
en su lirio. Paz, jazminero de cerezas, ya no herís
mi búsqueda. Me elevo dentro de mí hacia mí misma en brisa.
Me quedo aquí entre mi silencio y la luz, aquí ante la vida,
aquí contigo, mi dicha, mi morada de trigo y mi hambre.
Mi hambre, círculo a círculo hacia arriba, mi hambre yegua, mi hambre
hambre. Puedo descansar en mis manos, las hojas son nuevas,
puedo reposar en mi verso, puedo nombrar la medida
con mis dedos, noche a noche, luna, con mi lluvia hacia el centro.
Puedo decir: exceso de jilguero en las cumbres, exceso
de belleza en el lienzo, ausencia de no apresarte en mi dicha.
Tal vez, dolor y dicha. Tal vez, monte y sombra de
    los montes.
Tal vez, entré en mi corazón y la flauta se quebró en ramas
que ardieron como lana y luz, y yo ardí tres veces en el tiempo:
negué el aire y el agua, y no negué la rosa, ¿a qué evitarlo
si era necesario, si era exacto doler más en la rosa
para amar más y decir más y saber más en el silencio?
Me lavé en brisa el dolor, cancionero, me lavé en la brisa
las manos que me sostenían y el humo que me negaba.
No, cuerpo mío, no te negué nunca, y me bañé dos veces
en la misma brisa y dos veces en la misma agua, las aguas
que regresan a su origen y cierran lo abierto en la fuente.
Dos veces en la misma brisa y dos veces en la misma agua:
la de la vida y la del té, origen de la vida en el alma.
Dos veces en el mismo amor: soledad, tiempo en flor azul.
Serenidad, ¡qué difícil hallarte en el fruto sereno!,
Y me elevo siendo sueño de loto y rosas en los sueños.

Lotus and Rose in the Blue Flower

Christmas oratorio. Order of the universe and order
of the lotus in the light of the rose, of life over the lotus.
Memory and my mouth meet, the dark descends and I rise
like the breeze, like peace, or plenitude. I rise like a lake to the east
of the source, bread, plenitude. Transcendence no longer wounds.
Oratorio of the universe, the pine trees are words and fire,
air pools in the wind and water holds still
in its iris. Peace, jasmine bowl of cherries no longer wound
what I seek. Inside myself I rise tilting selfward in the breeze.
I remain between my silence and the light, here before life,
here with you, my happiness, my dwelling of wheat and my hunger.
My rising hunger, circle after circle, my mare hunger, my hunger
hunger. I can rest in my hands, the leaves are new,
I can rest in my poetry, I can name dimensions
with my fingers, night by night, the moon, with my rain the center.
I can say: too many goldfinch at the top, too much
beauty in the canvas, the blankness of you eluding my happiness.
Maybe, grief and good fortune. Maybe, mountain and the shadow of
    mountains.
Maybe, I saw my heart, the flute broke into branches
burning like wool and light, and I burned time in threes:
I refused air and water but not the rose, what is the point in avoiding it
if it was absolutely necessary, precisely, to feel more pain in the rose
to love more, to say more and to know more in silence?
I bathed pain, a book of songs, in the breeze, I bathed in the breeze
the hands that sustained me, the smoke that undid me.
No, dear body, I never denied you. I bathed twice
in the same breeze and twice in the same water, the waters
that return to their origin encircling the open fountain.
Twice in the same breeze and twice in the same water:
of life and tea, origin of life in the soul.
Twice in the same love: solitude, time in the blue flower.
Serenity, how hard it is to find you in the serene fruit!
And I rise, being the lotus dream and roses in dreams.

Todo huele a silencio

Y es invierno, y el verbo arde lento y breve como el perfume,
y contemplo, ausencia de conocimiento, el mimbre en la lengua
del ruiseñor, todo se hace eterno, el dulce sauce en el verbo
y todo se hace claro, con esa claridad del silencio,
orden de los sentidos, con esa claridad de la lluvia
sobre el sonido, o esa claridad de lo eterno en la encina.
Invierno, y la contemplación arde lenta como el almendro
en flor, y el universo huele a lluvia, a piedra en el silencio,
a yegua de pan y a luz, y a silencio sonoro en la lengua
del viento, viento en la hierba, viento en el centro de la escarcha,
en la huella del verbo que deja olor a huerta y a manos,
un olor a belleza, contemplación, un olor a tierra.
Dadle agua al almendro, dadle agua a la luz, avena a la piedra,
dadle agua al silencio, avena a la contemplación de la piedra,
agua a la luz, que toda sabiduría está en el comienzo;
dadle avena y agua al silencio, avena a la contemplación,
que esa es mi serenidad, que esa es la piedra de mis sentidos,
la piedra de mi tiempo en los muros, la piedra de mis sueños.
Contemplación, libro de rosal y loto, hoja de abedul
y acacia . . . encuentro el silencio, encuentro la luz en la belleza . . .
y el verbo arde en piedra blanca, y yo soy cereza, piedra y viento,
y soy verde tierra de encina y encina del ruiseñor
y trigo en el ciervo, fuego de aire y de agua, y fuego en el sauce.
Contemplo, conocimiento, te contemplo y me oculto y salgo,
y la piedra huele a centro y el centro a clara luz de invierno,
tiempo de los sentidos, tiempo de lo eterno en los sentidos.
Conciliación en el aire. Contemplo con el contemplar
del ser, con el ser de la mirada en los campos y en los cuerpos,
con el viento que eleva mis hojas y me rodea el nombre.
Contemplo, y no me encuentras, contemplación, que tengo por ojos
sol y luna, y las manos en talo de trigo son el medio
para juntar las manos sin principio ni fin, sin escarcha.
Contemplo, y me encuentras, contemplación, en mis ojos de viento
y chopo, soledad de hombro al alba, voz que roza el silencio,
en mis manos de piedra, cereza y sosiego, que se abrasan.
Es invierno, el verbo arde sereno y todo huele a silencio.

Everything Smells Like Silence

So it is winter, the word burns slow and brief like perfume,
and I contemplate (absence of knowing) the wickered tongue
of the nightingale. Everything turns eternal, the sweet willowed word,
and everything turns clear, with that clarity of silence,
order of the senses, with that clarity of rain
upon sound, or the clarity of the eternal in the evergreen oak.
Winter, and contemplation burns slow like the flowering
almond tree, and the universe smells like rain, like a stone in silence,
like a mare, like bread and light, like a sound of silence on the tongue
of the wind, wind in the grass, wind inside frost,
in the trace of the word that leaves a scent of garden and hands,
a scent of beauty, contemplation, a scent of earth.
Give water to the almond tree, give water to the light, oats to the stone,
give water to the silence, oats to the calm stone,
water to the light, all wisdom is in beginnings.
Give oats and water to silence, oats to contemplation,
for this is my serenity, these are the stones of my senses,
the stones of my time in the walls, the stones of my dreams.
Contemplation, book of the wild rose and lotus, birch leaf
and acacia . . . I find silence, I find the light in beauty,
and the word burns in white stone, and I am cherry, stone and wind.
I am the oak's green earth and the nightingale's oak
and wheat in the deer, fire of air and water, and fire in the willow.
I contemplate comprehension, yes you, I hide, then leave,
and stone smells like the inner core and the core like the clear light of winter,
time of the senses, time of the eternal in the senses.
A gathering in the air. I contemplate with all the contemplation
of being, being that looks at fields and bodies,
with the wind lifting my leaves and making a ring of my name.
I contemplate, but you cannot find me, contemplation. For eyes
I have sun and moon, and hands on the stalk of wheat
join to hands without beginning or end or frost.
I contemplate, and you find me, contemplation, in the wind and poplar
of my eyes, the shoulder's solitude at dawn, the voice that skims silence,
in my hands of stone, cherry and calm, catching fire.
It is winter, the word burns serene and everything smells like silence.

Coda:

Con el corazón desmesurado me tiendo en la luz

Con el corazón desmesurado, me traes el verano
ahora en un agosto sin cifras, tengo la yegua en la lengua
para decir, para callar, para amar, para que la yegua
vuelva a mi cuerpo, consagración, para que mi cuerpo vuelva
peregrino de sauces a la acacia que un día fue luz,
mi palabra o silencio de palabras con sólo el sonido
de sus ramas por conciencia, y por conciencia la sed del agua.
Silencio. Es Irene en los campos, hierba de Getsemaní.
Los sentidos. ¿Recuerdas en mi recuerdo aquel cielo azul,
la noche atravesada por el deseo o el melocotón
verde en la línea escrita y la vida pendiendo del sueño
y la alta manzana de los sueños rodando en la conciencia?
El otro, lo otro, el yo, la soledad,
rostros sin mito de la misma flecha,
del mismo aire.
Son otros los sueños. Me traes el verano en soledad,
silencio para que renazca, y la yegua roza la lengua,
y la palabra a la lengua, consagración, búho despierto
y mar dormido, y yo despierta para cuanto permanece.
¿Es eso la vida, la uva fatigada? Buen día, alma mía,
buenos días, campos, que me dejáis la memoria en las manos,
buenos días, manos, que recogéis de los campos los ojos
del lenguaje, mis ojos deseantes con piel de manzana,
hueso de luna, y tallo de mieses. Buenos días, angustia.
¿Es eso el amor, el habla en el pan? Buenos días, amor.
Con el corazón desmesurado, me traes el verano
y aquí está el yo, mitad agosto, mitad yegua, mitad lengua,
y la yegua busca la lengua, tristeza de carne y agua,
y la palabra, vida, hunde su flor azul en la memoria:
una acacia de luz rompe la piel del habla y la uva al alba
y yo amanezco en paz, búho ciego contemplando la vida.

With a Boundless Heart I Stretch out in the Light

With a boundless heart, you bring me summer
in endless harvest. I have the mare now, on the tongue
so I can speak, remain silent, love, so the mare
will return to my body, consecrated, for my body to return
strange as willow to the acacia that once was light,
my words or the silence of words with only the sound
of branches knowing, and the thirst of water knowing.
Silence. It is Irene in the fields, the grass of Gethsemane.
The senses. Do you remember that blue sky in my memory,
the night pierced by desire or the green
peach in the written line, life hanging from a dream
and the apple in dreams falling high into consciousness?
The other, what is other, the self, solitude,
faces stripped of myth from the same arrow,
the same air.
The dreams changed. You bring me summer in solitude,
the rebirth of silence, and the mare brushes against the tongue,
and the word against the tongue, consecrated, the owl is awake
and the sea asleep, and I am awake for everything permanent.
Is that life, the exhausted vine? Good morning, soul,
good morning, fields, leaving me memory in my hands,
good morning, hands, gathering in fields the eyes
of language, my eyes of desire with the apple's skin,
the bones of the moon and the stalks of corn. Good morning, anguish.
Is that love, the bread of words? Good morning, love.
With the heart boundless, you bring me summer
and here is the self, the part of harvest, mare, tongue,
and the mare seeks the tongue, the sadness of flesh and water,
and the word, life, plunges the blue flower in memory:
an acacia of light breaks the skin of speech and the vine at dawn
and I am dawn in peace, the blind owl contemplating life.

¿Qué la eternidad? Sólo conozco la carencia

Sólo sé que el agua conduce al agua, y a la piedra negra,
primordial, que del liquen nacen luna y tulipán dorado,
y sé que conozco la carencia en estado blanco y puro.
Sólo sé que esta tarde existe, y es hermosa, y es memoria
de encina, y que la armonía es correr, sin moverse, hacia el agua
blanca de los pájaros, hacia el manantial blanco del agua
quebrada en la antorcha, hacia el alma atravesada por los dedos
del amor que se tiende en el alma con sus ocas salvajes.
Sé que el amor es contemplación de la luz, eternidad,
y que este ser en paz es no tiempo, y tiempo de los helechos,
tal vez tiempo del té que sube a la tormenta para oír
el silencio, para decir sí a la carencia que nos lleva
a lo absoluto, sí a la nube que, dormida, abre los montes.

What About Eternity? I Know Only Lack

I only know that water leads to water, and to black, primordial
stone, that the moon and yellow tulip are born of lichen.
I know that I know absence in its pure, white state.
I only know this afternoon exists, and it is beautiful, this memory
of oak, and harmony is a running, without moving, toward the white
water of birds, toward the white stream of water
broken in torch light, toward the soul crossed by fingers
of love that stretches out in the soul with its wild geese.
I know that love is contemplation of the light, eternity,
and that this being in peace is not time, the time of bracken,
perhaps the time of tea rising in the storm to hear
silence, to say yes to the lack that takes us
to the absolute, yes to the sleeping cloud that opens mountains.

Aunque todo se incumpla, se cumple el aire

Aunque todo se incumpla, se cumple este rumor de ceniza
que ha sido brasa, que es brasa todavía si alzo una rosa
en su centro, si la ausento de mí, salvación, para a mí
volverla, hecho de cintura, gesto de altura, alma del aire.

Though Nothing is Fulfilled, the Air is Filled

Though nothing is fulfilled, this rumor of ash is filled,
was once a burning coal, is still a burning coal if I raise a rose
in its center, or take it away, saving grace, and return
it to me as a waist, a sign rising high, a soul of air.

Creación del silencio

Cuánta música en la duda, elegía del pan contra la hoja,
elegía de la mano en lo diverso, mano entre el alma
y el verbo, agua que huele a quebradura, ¿no oléis el silencio?,
¿no oléis la boca del ruiseñor en la celosía, a cidra
en lo cierto, en lo cernido, en lo sereno?, ¿no oléis a amor
en el lienzo, contra el té, al otro lado del verbo, a este lado
del silencio?, ¿no oléis a mimbre en la paloma hasta que su ojo
y su mejilla es cauce del ciruelo, y su pulso, aguas claras?
Las oscuras aguas del búho oscuro en las noches sin luna
huelen a ceguera, a rodilla en la sombra, a dolor sin peso,
y mi alma huele a agua y quebradura. ¿Oléis mi hambre
    en la ceguera?
Y descansé hasta que la mejilla fue cauce del ciruelo.

Creation of Silence

Such music there is in doubt, bread's elegy against the blade,
the hand's elegy in diversity, hand amid the soul
and word, water that smells like breaking, do you smell the silence?
Do you smell the nightingale's mouth in the window's lattice, like cider
in sifted certainty, in serenity? Do you smell love
in the canvas, facing the tea, on the other side of the verb, on this side
of silence? Do you smell willow in the dove till its eye
and cheek are the plum tree's riverbed, and its pulse, clear water?
The dark waters of the dark owl in moonless nights
smell like blindness, a knee in shadow, weightless pain,
and my soul smells like water breaking. Do you smell my hunger
    in the blindness?
And I rested till my cheek was the plum tree's riverbed.

Cuando algo tiende a lo absoluto

Nos hiciste de arcilla, Señor, con una hierba en el centro
por alma, con un búho en el centro por angustia, con un río
por diálogo y desazón y coraje de arrayán en el pórtico
del gesto, y tú eres hierba, ¿cómo rozar la hierba con la hierba?

Y la hierba debe hundir su despertar en el árbol dormido.

When Something Tends to the Absolute

You made us from clay, Lord, with grass in the center
for a soul, with an owl in the center for anguish, with a river
for dialogue and discomfort and the myrtle's spirit in the portal's
sign, and you are the grass. How to graze the grass with grass?

And grass must plunge awake into the sleeping tree.